I AM, I AM, I AM

I AM, I AM, I AM

Seventeen Brushes
with Death

MAGGIE O'FARRELL

ALFRED A. KNOPF
New York · Toronto   2018

THIS IS A BORZOI BOOK
PUBLISHED BY ALFRED A. KNOPF
AND ALFRED A. KNOPF CANADA

Copyright © 2017 by Maggie O'Farrell
All rights reserved. Published in the United States by
Alfred A. Knopf, a division of Penguin Random House LLC,
New York, and in Canada by Alfred A. Knopf Canada, a division
of Penguin Random House Canada Limited, Toronto. Originally
published in hardcover in Great Britain by Tinder Press, an
imprint of Headline Publishing Group,
a Hachette UK Company, London, in 2017.

www.aaknopf.com
www.penguinrandomhouse.ca

Knopf, Borzoi Books, and the colophon are registered trademarks
of Penguin Random House LLC.
Knopf Canada and colophon are registered trademarks
of Penguin Random House Canada Limited.

Library of Congress Cataloging-in-Publication Data
Names: O'Farrell, Maggie, 1972–author.
Title: I am, I am, I am : seventeen brushes with death /
Maggie O'Farrell.
Description: First edition. | New York : Alfred A. Knopf, 2018.
Identifies: LCCN 2017028597 (print) | LCCN 2017037164 (ebook) |
ISBN 9780525520221 (hardcover) | ISBN 9780525520238 (ebook)
Subjects: LCSH: O'Farrell, Maggie, 1972– | Novelists, Irish—20th
century—Biography.
Classification: LCC PR6065.F36 (ebook) | LCC PR6065.F36 z46
2018 (print) | DDC 823/.914 [B]—dc23
LC record available at https://lccn.loc.gov/2017028597

Library and Archives Canada Cataloguing in Publication data
is available upon request
ISBN 978-0-7352-7411-2 | eBook ISBN 978-0-7352-7412-9

Front-of-jacket illustration by Gina Triplett
Jacket design by Kelly Blair

Manufactured in the United States of America
Published February 6, 2018
Second Printing, February 2018

336140805561656

for my children

In some cases, names, appearances and locations have been changed to protect the identities of those who may not have wanted to be written about in a book.

Certain sections of this book originally appeared, in other forms, in the following publications:

—parts of "Daughter," in *Guardian Weekend,* May 2016

—parts of "Baby and Bloodstream," in *Good Housekeeping,* February 2007

—parts of "Abdomen," in the *Guardian,* May 2004

I took a deep breath and listened to the old brag of my heart. I am, I am, I am.

Sylvia Plath, *The Bell Jar*

Contents

NECK

1990

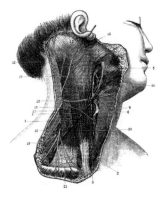

On the path ahead, stepping out from behind a boulder, a man appears.

We are, he and I, on the far side of a dark tarn that lies hidden in the bowl-curved summit of this mountain. The sky is a milky blue above us; no vegetation grows this far up so it is just me and him, the stones and the still black water. He straddles the narrow track with both booted feet and he smiles.

I realise several things. That I passed him earlier, farther down the glen. We greeted each other, in the amiable yet brief manner of those on a country walk. That, on this remote stretch of path, there is no one near enough to hear me call. That he has been waiting for me: he has planned this whole thing, carefully, meticulously, and I have walked into his trap.

I see all this, in an instant.

This day—a day on which I nearly die—began early for me, just after dawn, my alarm clock leaping into a rattling dance beside the bed. I had to pull on my uniform, leave the caravan and tiptoe down some stone steps into a

3

deserted kitchen, where I flicked on the ovens, the coffee machines, the toasters, where I sliced five large loaves of bread, filled the kettles, folded forty paper napkins into open-petalled orchids.

I have just turned eighteen, and I have pulled off an escape. From everything: home, school, parents, exams, the waiting for results. I have found a job, far away from everyone I know, in what is advertised as a "holistic, alternative retreat" at the base of a mountain.

I serve breakfast, I clear away breakfast, I wipe tables, I remind guests to leave their keys. I go into the rooms, I make the beds, I change the sheets, I tidy. I pick up clothes and towels and books and shoes and essential oils and meditation mats from the floor. I learn, from the narratives inherent in possessions left strewn around the bedrooms, that people are not always what they seem. The rather sententious, exacting man who insists on a specific table, certain soap, an entirely fat-free milk has a penchant for cloud-soft cashmere socks and exuberantly patterned silk underwear. The woman who sits at dinner with her precisely buttoned blouse and lowered eyelids and growing-out perm has a nocturnal avatar who will don S&M outfits of an equestrian bent: human bridles, tiny leather saddles, a slender but vicious silver whip. The couple from London, who seem wonderingly, enviably

4

perfect—they hold manicured hands over dinner, they take laughing walks at dusk, they show me photos of their wedding—have a room steeped in sadness, in hope, in grief. Ovulation kits clutter their bathroom shelves. Fertility drugs are stacked on their nightstands. These I don't touch, as if to impart the message, I didn't see this, I am not aware, I know nothing.

All morning, I sift and organise and ease the lives of others. I clear away human traces, erasing all evidence that they have eaten, slept, made love, argued, washed, worn clothes, read newspapers, shed hair and skin and bristle and blood and toenails. I dust, I walk the corridors, trailing the vacuum cleaner behind me on a long leash. Then, around lunchtime, if I'm lucky, I have four hours before the evening shift to do whatever I want.

So I have walked up to the lake, as I often do during my time off, and today, for some reason, I have decided to take the path right around to the other side. Why? I forget. Maybe I finished my tasks earlier that day, maybe the guests had been less untidy than usual and I'd got out of the guesthouse before time. Maybe the clear, sun-bright weather has lured me from my usual path.

I have also had no reason, at this point in my life, to distrust the countryside. I have been to self-defence lessons, held at the community centre in the small Scottish seaside town where I spent my teens. The teacher, a barrel-shaped man in a judo suit, would put scenarios to us with startling Gothic relish. Late at night and you're coming out of a pub, he would say, eyeing us one by one from beneath his excessively sprouting eyebrows, and a huge bloke lunges out from an alleyway and grabs you. Or: you're in a narrow corridor in a nightclub and some drunk shoves you up against a wall. Or: it's dark, it's foggy, you're waiting at the traffic lights and someone seizes your bag strap and pushes you to the ground. These narratives of peril always ended with the same question, put to us with slightly gloating rhetoric: so, what do you do?

We practised reversing our elbows into the throats of our imaginary assailants, rolling our eyes as we did so because we were, after all, teenage girls. We took it in turns to rehearse the loudest shout we could. We repeated, dutifully, dully, the weak points in a male body: eye, nose, throat, groin, knee. We believed we had it covered, that we could take on the lurking stranger, the drunk assailant, the bag-snatching mugger. We were sure we'd be able to break their grip, bring up our knee, scratch at their eyes with our nails; we reckoned we could find an exit out of these alarming yet oddly thrilling synopses. We were taught to make noise, to attract attention, to yell, POLICE. We also, I think, imbibed a clear message. Alleyway, nightclub, pub, bus-stop, traffic lights: the danger was urban. In the country, or in rural towns like ours—where there were no nightclubs, no alleyways and no traffic lights, even—things like this did not happen. We were free to do as we pleased.

And yet here is this man, high up a mountain, blocking my way, waiting for me.

It seems important not to show my fear, to play along. So I keep walking, keep putting one foot in front of the other. If I turn and run, he could catch up with me in seconds and there would be something so exposing, so final about running. It would uncover to us both what this situation is; it would bring things to a head. The only option seems to be to carry on, to pretend that this is perfectly normal.

"Hello again," he says to me, and his gaze slides over my face, my body, my bare, muddy legs. It is a glance more assessing than lascivious, more calculating than lustful: it is the look of a man working something out, planning the logistics of a deed.

I cannot meet his gaze, I cannot look at him directly, not quite, but I am aware of narrow-set eyes, a considerable height, ivory-coloured incisors, fists gripping his rucksack straps.

I have to clear my throat to say, "Hi." I think I nod. I turn myself sideways so as to step past him: a sharp mix of fresh sweat, leather from his rucksack, some kind of chemical-heavy shaving oil that seems distantly familiar.

I am past him, I am walking away, the path is open before me. He has, I note, chosen for his ambush the apex of the hike: I have climbed and climbed, and it is at this point that I will start to descend the mountain, to my guesthouse, to my evening shift, to work, to life. It's all downhill from here.

I am careful to use strides that are confident, purposeful, but not frightened. I am not frightened: I say this to myself, over the oceanic roar of my pulse. Perhaps, I think, I am free, perhaps I have misread the situation. Perhaps it's perfectly normal to lie in wait for young girls on remote paths and then let them go.

I am eighteen. Just. I know almost nothing.

I do know, though, that he is right behind me. I can hear the tread of his boots, the swishing movement of his trouser fabric—some kind of breathable, all-weather affair.

And here he is again, falling into step beside me. He walks closely, intimately, his arm at my shoulder, the way a friend might, the way I walked home from school with classmates.

8

"Lovely day," he says, looking into my face.

I keep my head bowed. "Yes," I say, "it is."

"Very hot. I might go for a swim."

There is something peculiar about his diction, I realise, as we tread the path together with rapid, synchronised steps. His words halt mid-syllable; his *r*s are soft, his *t*s over-enunciated, his tone flat, almost expressionless. Maybe he's slightly "touched," as the expression goes, like the man who used to live down the road from us. He hadn't thrown anything out since the war and his front garden was overrun, like Sleeping Beauty's castle, with ivy. We used to try to guess what some of the leaf-draped objects were: a car, a fence, a motorbike? He wore knitted hats and patterned tank tops and too-small once-smart suits that were coated with cat-hair. If it was raining, he slung a bin liner over his shoulders. Sometimes he would come to our door with a zipped bag full of kittens for us to play with; other times he would be drunk, livid, wild-eyed and ranting about lost postcards, and my mother would have to take him by the arm and lead him home. "Stay there," she would say to us, "I'll be back in a tick," and she'd be off down the pavement with him.

Maybe, I think, with a flood of relief, that's all this means. This man might be like our old neighbour: eccentric, different, now long dead, his house cleared and

I AM, I AM, I AM

sanitised, the ivy hacked down and burnt. Perhaps I should be kind, as my mother was. I should be compassionate.

I turn to him then, as we walk together, in rapid step, beside the lake. I even smile.

"A swim," I say. "That sounds nice."

He answers by putting his binocular strap around my neck.

A day or so later, I walk into the police station in the nearby town. I wait in line with people reporting lost wallets, stray dogs, scraped cars.

The policeman at the desk listens, head cocked to the side. "Did he hurt you?" is his first question. "This man, did he touch you, hit you, proposition you? Did he do or say anything improper?"

"No," I say, "not exactly, but—"

"But what?"

"He would have done," I say. "He was going to."

The man looks me up and down. I'm wearing patched cut-offs, numerous silver hoops through the cartilage of my ears, tattered sneakers, a T-shirt with a picture of a dodo and the words "Have you seen this bird?" on it. I have a mane—there isn't really any other word to describe it—of wild hair into which a guest, a serene-faced Dutch woman, who had travelled to the guesthouse with her harp and a felting kit, has woven beads and feathers. I look like what I am: a teenager who has been living alone for the first time, in a caravan, in a forest, in the middle of nowhere.

"So," the policeman says, leaning heavily on his papers, "you went for a walk, you met a man, you walked with him, he was a bit peculiar, but then you got home okay. Is that what you're telling me?"

"He put," I say, "the strap of his binoculars around my neck."

"And then what?"

"He . . ." I stop. I hate this man with his thick eyebrows, his beery paunch, his impatient stubby fingers. I hate him more, perhaps, than the man beside the tarn. "He showed me some ducks on the lake."

The policeman doesn't even try to hide his smile. "Right," he says, and shuts his book with a snap. "Sounds terrifying."

How should I have articulated to this policeman that I could sense the urge for violence radiating off the man, like heat off a stone? I have been over and over that moment at the desk in the police station, asking myself, was there anything I could have done differently, anything

I might have said that would have changed what happened next?

I could have said: I want to see your supervisor, I want to see the person in charge. I would do this now, age forty-three, but then? It didn't occur to me it was possible.

I could have said: Listen to me, that man didn't hurt me but he will hurt someone else. Please find him before he does.

I could have said that I have an instinct for the onset of violence. That, for a long time, I seemed to incite it in others for reasons I never quite understood. If, as a child, you are struck or hit, you will never forget that sense of your own powerlessness and vulnerability, of how a situation can turn from benign to brutal in the blink of an eye, in the space of a breath. That sensibility will run in your veins, like an antibody. You learn fairly quickly to recognise the approach of these sudden acts against you: that particular pitch or vibration in the atmosphere. You develop antennae for violence and, in turn, you devise a repertoire of means to divert it.

The school I went to seemed steeped in it. The threat, like smoke, filled the corridors, the halls, the classrooms, the aisles between desks. Heads were smacked, ears were gripped, chalk dusters were thrown, with smarting accuracy; one teacher had the habit of picking up kids he didn't like by the waistbands of their trousers and launching them at the walls. I can still recall the sound of child cranium hitting Victorian tile.

For the worst offences, boys were sent to the headmistress, where they were given the cane. Girls got the dap. I used to look at my daps—those black canvas shoes with a horseshoe of elastic across the front that we were made to wear when climbing over gym horses—and in particular their greyish rippled soles and imagine the impact: rubber on exposed flesh.

The headmistress was an object of awed fear. Her sinewy neck and bird-claw hands. Her scarves skewered to sweaters with a silver pin. Her office with its dark walls and wine-coloured rug. If called there to demonstrate skills with coded reading books, I would look down at this rug and picture having to stand there, my skirt pulled up, awaiting my fate, bracing myself for the blow.

It filtered down to the pupils, of course. Chinese burns were particularly popular, when the skin of your forearm could be wrung like a damp cloth into vivid ellipses. Hairpulling, toe-crushing, head-locking, finger-twisting: there was a large and ever-expanding range at the bullies' disposal. I had the misfortune of not speaking with a local accent, of being able to read before I got there, of having an appearance that, I was informed, was abnormal, offensive, unacceptable in some way, of wearing skirts that had been taken up and let down too many times, of being sickly and missing large chunks of school, of stammering whenever called on to speak, of having shoes that weren't patent leather and so on. I remember a boy in my class trapping me behind the brick shelter and wordlessly yanking me up by the straps of my sundress until they cut into my underarms. He and I never referred to this incident again. I remember an older girl with a glossy dark fringe materialising from the playtime crowd to grind my face into the bark of a tree. In my first term at comprehensive school, in the middle of a chemistry lesson, I was punched in the face by a twelve-year-old skinhead. If I probe my upper lip with the tip of my tongue, I can still feel the scar.

So, when the man put the binocular strap around my neck, even though he was saying something about wanting to show me a flock of eider ducks, I knew what came next. I could smell it, I could almost see it there, thickening and glittering in the air between us. This man was just another in a long line of bullies who had taken exception to my accent or my shoes or godknowswhat—I had long since stopped caring—and he was going to hurt me. He meant to inflict harm, rain it down on my head, and there was nothing I could do about it.

I decided I must play along with the birdwatching game. I knew that this was my only hope. You can't confront a bully; you can't call them out; you can't let them know that you know, that you see them for what they are.

I glanced through the binoculars for the length of a single heartbeat. Oh, I said, eider ducks, goodness, and I ducked down and away, out of the circle of that strap. He came after me, of course he did, with that length of black leather, intending to lasso me again, but by this time I was facing him, I was smiling at him, gabbling about eider ducks and how interesting they were, did eiderdowns used to be made of them, is that where the name came from, were they filled with eider-duck feathers? They were? How fascinating. Tell me more, tell me everything you know about ducks, about birds, about birdwatching, goodness, how knowledgeable you are, you must go birdwatching a lot. You do? Tell me some more about it, about the most unusual bird you've ever seen, tell me while we walk because is that the time, I really must be going now, down the hill, because I have to start my shift, yes, I work just there—you see those chimneys? That's the place. It's quite close, isn't it? There will be people waiting for me. Sometimes if I'm late they'll come out to look for me, yes, my boss, he'll be waiting. He walks up here all the time too, all the staff do, he knows I'm out here, he certainly does, he knows exactly where, I told him myself, he'll be out looking for me any minute now, he'll be just around that corner. Sure, we can walk this way, and while we do, why don't you tell me some more about birdwatching, yes, please, I'd like that but I really must rush because they are waiting.

Two weeks later, a police car drives up the winding track to the guesthouse and two people get out. I see them from an upper window, where I'm wrestling pillows into their cases. I know straight away what they are doing here, why they have come, so even before I hear someone calling my name, I am walking down the stairs to meet them.

These two are nothing like the policeman at the station. They are in suits, their demeanours serious, focused. They proffer badges and documents to my boss, Vincent, with faces that are still with practised, skilled neutrality.

They want to talk to me in private so Vincent shows them into an unoccupied room. He comes in with us because he is a good man and I am only a few years older than his own children, whose cries and shouts can be heard from the back lawn.

I sit on a bed I made that morning, and the policeman

sits at an ornamental wicker table where some guests like to take their morning tea; the policewoman seats herself next to me on the bed.

Vincent hovers in the background, muttering mistrustfully, pretending to adjust a crystal hanging at the window, to wipe non-existent dust off the mantelpiece, to rattle the fire-irons in the grate. He is a former flower child, a Haight-Ashbury survivor, and has a low opinion of what he calls "the fuzz."

The police ignore him, in a polite but preoccupied way. They are interested, the woman tells me, in a man I encountered recently on a walk. Would I be able to tell them exactly what happened?

So I do. I start at the beginning, describing how I passed him early on the hike, how he headed off in the opposite direction, then somehow appeared ahead of me. "I don't know how he did that," I say, "because there isn't a short-cut, or not one that I know of." They nod and nod, listening with a measured intensity, encouraging me to go on. Their eyes never leave my face: I have their absolute attention. When I get to the part about the binoculars strap, they stop nodding. They stare at me, both of them, their eyes unblinking. It is a strange, congested moment. I don't think any of us breathes.

"A binoculars strap?" the man asks.

"Yes," I say.

"And he put it around your neck?"

I nod. They look away, look down; the woman makes a note of something in her book.

Would I be willing, she asks, as she hands me a folder, to take a look at some photographs and let them know if I see him there?

At this point, my boss interrupts. He can't not. "You don't have to say anything, you know, you don't. She doesn't have to say anything."

The policewoman is putting up her hand to silence him, just as I am placing my index finger on a photograph.

"That's him," I say.

The detectives look. The woman notes something again in her book. The man thanks me; he takes the folder.

"He killed someone," I say to them, "didn't he?"

They exchange an unreadable glance but say nothing.

"He strangled someone. With his binoculars strap." I look from one to the other and we know, we all know. "Didn't he?"

From across the room, Vincent swears softly. Then he walks over and gives me his handkerchief.

The girl who died was twenty-two. She was from New Zealand and was backpacking around Europe with her boyfriend. He was unwell that day so had stayed behind at their hostel while she went off on a hike, alone. She was raped, strangled, then buried in a shallow pit. Her body was discovered three days later, not far from the path where I had been walking.

I only know all this because I read about it in the local newspaper the following week: the police wouldn't tell me. I saw a headline in a newsagent's window, went in to buy a paper, and there was her face, looking out at me from the front page. She had light-coloured hair, held back in a band, a freckled face, a wide, guileless smile.

It wouldn't be an exaggeration to say that I think about her, if not every day then most days. I am aware of her life, which was cut off, curtailed, snipped short, whereas mine, for whatever reason, was allowed to run on.

I never knew if they caught him, if he was convicted, sentenced, imprisoned. I had the distinct feeling, during the interview, that those detectives were on to him, that they had him, that they just needed my corroboration. Maybe the DNA samples were incontrovertible. Maybe he confessed. Maybe there were other witnesses, other victims, other near-misses, who gave evidence in court: I was never asked and was too green or, I suspect, too shocked to pursue the matter, to call the police and say, what happened, did you catch him, has he been put away? I left the area not long afterwards so can never be certain. All this happened long before a time of ubiquitous and instantly available news. I can find no sign, no trace of this crime on the internet, despite numerous searches.

I don't know why he spared me but not her. Did she panic? Did she try to run? Did she scream? Did she make the mistake of alerting him to the monster he was?

For a long time, I dreamt about the man on the path. He would appear in a variety of disguises, but always with his rucksack and binoculars. Sometimes, in the murk and confusion of a dream, I would recognise him only by these accoutrements and I would think, oh, it's you again, is it? You've come back?

It is a story difficult to put into words, this. I never tell it, in fact, or never have before. I told no one at the time, not my friends, not my family: there seemed no way to translate what had happened into grammar and syntax. I have, now I think about it, only ever told one person, and that was the man I would eventually marry, and it only came out years after we first met. I told him one evening in Chile, as we sat together in the refectory of a travellers' hostel. The expression on his face was one of such deep, visceral shock that I knew I would probably never tell it again, verbally, in my lifetime.

What happened to that girl, and what so nearly happened to me, is not something to be lightly articulated, moulded into anecdote, formed into a familiar spoken groove to be told and retold over a dinner table or on the telephone, passed from teller to teller. It is instead a tale of horror, of evil, of our worst imaginings. It is a story to be kept battened down in some wordless, unvisited dark place. Death brushed past me on that path, so close that I could feel its touch, but it seized that other girl and thrust her under.

I still cannot bear anyone to touch my neck: not my husband, not my children, not a kindly doctor, who once wanted to check my tonsils. I flinch away before I even register why. I can't wear anything around it. Scarves, polo necks, choker necklaces, any top or blouse that applies pressure there: none of these will ever be for me.

My daughter recently pointed to the top of a hill, seen on our walk to school.

"Can we go up there?"

"Sure," I said, glancing up at the green summit.

"Just you and me?"

I was silent for a moment. "We can all go," I said. "The whole family."

Alert as ever to the moods of others, she immediately

caught the sense that I was holding something back. "Why not just you and me?"

"Because . . . everyone else would like to come too."

"But why not you and me?"

Because, I was thinking, because I cannot begin to say. Because I cannot articulate what dangers lie around corners for you, around twisting paths, around boulders, in the tangles of forests. Because you are six years old. Because there are people out there who want to hurt you and you will never know why. Because I haven't yet worked out how to explain these things to you. But I will.

LUNGS

1988

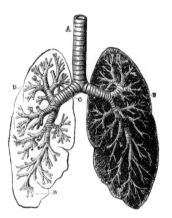

It is late, near midnight, and a group of teenagers are out at the end of the quay. The town lies across the bay, a necklace of lights strung along the sand. The harbour is a place where they congregate: it is always possible to find others of their kind here, without prior arrangement. Something of its liminal nature, its space between land and sea, seems to draw them, especially at night.

They are out late. They are bored, in that mind-shrivelling way peculiar to this stage in life. They are sixteen or thereabouts. They have just sat their first set of exams and are waiting for the results, waiting for the summer to be over, for the new school year to begin, waiting for their futures to take shape, waiting for their shifts to end, waiting for the tourists to leave, waiting, waiting. Some are waiting for bad haircuts to grow out, for their parents to allow them to drive or give them more money or clock their unhappiness, for the boy or girl they like to notice them, for the cassette tape they ordered at the music shop to arrive, for their shoes to wear out so they can be bought new ones, for the bus to arrive, for the phone to ring. They are, all of them, waiting because that is what teenagers who grow up in seaside towns do. They wait. For something to end, for something to begin.

Two of them have been out together, broken up, got back together. Some can drive but others haven't yet started. One smokes but mostly they don't. They are not the ones at school to do drugs or drink to excess or sleep around.

All of them have summer jobs, of varying descriptions, serving the tourists who clog the town in these months, like sand in a shoe. Two of the boys work as litter-pickers on the golf course; a girl serves ice-cream from the van at the beachfront.

One of these teenagers is me. I am working evenings as a waitress in a golfing lodge. As I sit there, on the cool volcanic stone of the harbour wall, feet dangling over the drop, I can catch the scent of the hotel on my hair—cigarettes, reheated food, chip-pan oil, the beer spilt on my cuff. The smell of catering and bars and other people's holidays.

When one of the other girls suggests jumping off the harbour wall into the water below, it doesn't make me particularly uneasy. There have been times, with other people, when it has been possible to feel the group dynamics shifting and tilting to a dangerous angle. If someone comes up with a dare or turns on another person or suggests something perilous, illegal or both, the evening can veer off course. The girl who demanded that we jump aboard a slow-moving goods train. The boy who climbed on top of a disused carousel, slipped and spent the rest of term in plaster. The girl who dropped lit matches into all the municipal rubbish bins along the seafront. The pair who let down the tyres and removed the windscreen wipers from the headmaster's car.

I tell my children about these things, now, and they look at me, wide-eyed. You did that? they ask. Not me, I say, but someone I was with. There will be times, I tell them, when you're teenagers and you're out and someone will suggest something that you know is a bad idea and you will have to make a choice whether to join in or leave. To go with the group or against it. To speak up, to speak out, to say, no, I don't think we should do that. No, I don't want this. No, I'm going home.

I have never found it difficult to abandon a group, to go against the alpha male or female. I have never much cared for gangs, for social tribes, for fitting in. I have known since I was very young that the in-crowd isn't my crowd; they are not my people. So it isn't that which propels me to unfold myself up there on the harbour wall, to scramble, then stand up in the light breeze blowing in off the sea and say: "I'll do it."

It is more a desire to do something—anything—that pulls me out of the repetitive mundanity of a sixteen-year-old's life. To differentiate this day from all the others in the endless chain of days I'm living through. It is a desire to immerse myself in the water, that other element, the dark and shifting shape at the base of the harbour wall: I can sense its depth, its mass, its cold, waiting power, even though I can't see it. To hope that it can remove the taint of the hotel, the dining room, the husbands who size me up when I ask for their dessert orders and say, in front of their simpering wives, "I think I'll have you." It is a job from which you come away soiled, queasy, stinking of the deep-fat fryer. It is a job in which you may be felt up by several members of a golfing party as you silver-serve them vegetables, and it takes everything in you not to invert the fork you're holding and drive it into their thick wrists. It is a job during which a chef might very easily drop his kitchen scrubs and waggle his hips at you, his dick disconcertingly pink and bald inside its nest of black hair, and you are meant to shriek and laugh. It is the older waitresses—the ones who do this full-time, for a living, not just as a summer job—who are allowed to pick up a napkin and slap it down on the dick in question and say, put that away and leave the lassie alone. It is a job in which the kitchen porter might get a fancy for taking a skinned oxtail and, because he has found out that you are a vegetarian, come up behind you as you are bending into the ice-cream freezer in the lightless outhouse and tie your wrists together with its cold, gelatinous length.

It is all these things and more that propel me to my feet. At sixteen, you can be so restless, so frustrated, so disgusted by everything that surrounds you that you are willing to leap off what is probably a fifteen-metre drop, in the dark, into a turning tide.

The sea is calm tonight. It roils with a smooth, oiled motion below us. I slip off my shoes. I don't look down.

The drop is faster than you might think. There is a rush of air, like a gush of wind through a suddenly opened door, and then I am enveloped in another world, swallowed by the sea.

My ears roar, my sinuses fill, my mouth and eyes sting with salt, my shirt floats up around me, like wings. I must have hit the water at an angle because one side of my body throbs. The water is black: an absolute dark, this, an ur-dark, aphotic, without a glimmer of light. I open and shut my eyes and there is no difference, no alteration.

I am still sinking, down and down, slower and slower, and I think that soon I will reach the bottom, that my feet will come into contact with silty sand and then I will be able to push off, push back, return to the surface, to my friends, to my life.

No sand can be felt. I pedal my feet, stretching out my toes like a ballet dancer—but nothing. I am still sinking, or at least I think I am. Surely it can't be this deep.

Enveloped in water, I realise something. My coordination, my sense of spatial orientation is not as it should be. A childhood illness has resulted in sustained damage, as neurologists have said, to those parts of my brain involved in movement and balance. The people up on the harbour don't know this: a move here a few years earlier has meant that they were spared the sight of me in a wheelchair, disabled, a special-needs case. I have impairment to a number of neurological functions, one of which is the ability to sense where things are or should be and my place among them. I have lost this unconscious function and I must rely instead on visual clues: proprioception, it's called, the ability I lack. So I can't reach out for a pen while talking to someone else. I need to stop, look, direct my hand, and only then can I connect palm with pen. If the visual clues are removed, for whatever reason, I am flummoxed, I am helpless, I am—in short—at sea.

It is also why, if I happen to fall into black, lightless

water late at night, I will have no sense of which way is up, no way of orienting myself towards air.

I have wondered, since, what was going on up there on the harbour wall. How long it took them to realise I wasn't resurfacing. Whether, after their initial whooping and cheering, they started chatting again, whether they fell silent after however many seconds, whether they watched the surface of the water for me to emerge. We didn't talk about it afterwards: it was too much for us, then, the danger too large, too close.

I flail about down there, beneath them all. I struggle one way, thinking it must be to the surface, then the other. At this point, your lungs start to burn, your pulse races, your heart tripping into an allegretto time signature, aiming to alert you to the situation, as if you haven't noticed that you are about to die. You have an urgent need to cough but you know you mustn't, you cannot. Your thoughts are monosemic: It's okay, it's okay, it's okay. And then: It's not okay, it's not okay, it's not.

There is nothing unique or special in a near-death experience. They are not rare; everyone, I would venture, has had them, at one time or another, perhaps without even realising it. The brush of a van too close to your bicycle, the tired medic who realises that a dosage ought to be checked one final time, the driver who has drunk too much and is reluctantly persuaded to relinquish the car keys, the train missed after sleeping through an alarm, the aeroplane not caught, the virus never inhaled, the assailant never encountered, the path not taken. We are, all of us, wandering about in a state of oblivion, borrowing our time, seizing our days, escaping our fates, slipping through loopholes, unaware of when the axe may fall. As Thomas Hardy writes of Tess Durbeyfield, "There was another date . . . that of her own death; a day which lay sly and unseen among all the other days of the year, giving no sign or sound when she annually passed over it; but not the less surely there. When was it?"

If you are aware of these moments, they will alter you. You can try to forget them, to turn away from them, to shrug them off, but they will have infiltrated you, whether you like it or not. They will take up residence inside you and become part of who you are, like a heart stent or a pin that holds together a broken bone.

Recently I was going through old boxes and files, looking for some faxes I had received in the 1990s. I came across a slew of other things: photos of people I had all but forgotten, birthday cards, Valentines, cinema stubs, train tickets, museum guides, maps of cities I once visited. I came across a letter, written to me by one of the boys at the harbour that night.

It was sent to my university address. He and I were, by that time, studying at opposite ends of the country, and school seemed a very long time ago. He wrote, in looping black ballpoint, that I had made him miserable at school: I would never commit to him, never agree to be his, always evaded him. We always got on well, he wrote, so why? Why wouldn't you be my girlfriend?

I remembered getting the letter; I remembered reading it as I walked to a seminar, my books and notes in my bicycle basket. I wrote back to him a few weeks later, saying that I was sorry, more than sorry, for making him unhappy. I had no idea, I wrote, you felt that way.

This, of course, isn't true. I must have known it before I read the letter and also while I replied to it, sitting at my university desk, with my pad of paper resting on my lecture notes, my library books, my unfinished essays.

It is this boy who comes in after me. I am still under the water and my muscles are tiring, my mind is beginning to drift. The boy is a committed water-skier, kayaker, dinghy-sailor: he spends most of his spare time in or on the sea. The bathroom at his house is always full of dripping, sandy wetsuits, which loom above the shower like hanged men. He has been a swimming champion, one of those adolescents who rise before dawn to do countless laps in the chlorinated blue of a pool. He goes off to things called galas at weekends and wins trophies.

It is he who looks at the tide, divines where I will have been dragged, dives in, resurfaces, dives again, resurfaces, dives a third time, finds me, seizes me under the arms, by the jaw. It is he who kicks and kicks until we break the surface. It is he who calls me a fucking idiot when we finally emerge, and he still holds me so tightly it's difficult for me to draw in the sudden air, and, as he scolds me, his face is furious, frightened, and something else as well.

As I write this, I think about the black water, the choking tar texture of it, its secret invisible pull. I think about the frantic grip of his hands. There was no mistaking what drove him into that freezing water, into the depths of the sea to haul me out. There was a reason it was him and not one of the others who jumped in after me. I knew it, as a sixteen-year-old. Of course I did. I knew it in the way we walked home afterwards, him several steps behind me, both of us shivering and wet, barefoot and arguing. I felt it in his anger, in the way he told me what might have happened to me, how the tides work by drawing out the water underneath the surface, how I could have been swept out to sea, how I must never do anything so stupid again. I sensed it in the way he watched me go up my garden path, as I slipped wordlessly away from him and disappeared behind my front door.

What I should have said was: you're right, it was a stupid thing to do. I should have said: the thing is, I have this compulsion for freedom, for a state of liberation. It is an urge so strong, so all-encompassing that it over-whelms everything else. I cannot stand my life as it is. I cannot stand to be here, in this town, in this school. I have to get away. I have to work and work so that I can leave, and only then can I create a life that will be liveable for me. I may appear flighty and capricious, talking to you one day, then retreating the next but, you see, I have to concentrate everything on freeing myself and nothing can get in my way. I cannot bear for anything or anyone to slow me down, distract me, fetter me. I should also have said: thank you.

Thank you, thank you.

SPINE, LEGS, PELVIS, ABDOMEN, HEAD

1977

As a child, I was an escapologist, a bolter. I ran, scarpered, dashed off, legged it whenever I had the chance. I hated to be held by the hand, to be restrained, tethered, expected to walk in an orderly fashion. I used to squirm free, twist away. I wanted nothing more than to be on the move, air rushing around me, in flight, the street or the garden or the park or the field reeling past. I wanted to know, wanted to see, what was around the next corner, beyond the bend. I still do.

I was perhaps four or five when I first got lost, which was what my mother always warned might happen, the logical conclusion to my struggling free, my running off. We had gone to a service in a chapel on an uninhabited island, a boat ride away from the coast of County Mayo, and I had lagged behind, running in zigzag formations, until I found myself alone. Fearsomely, unaccountably, thrillingly alone: a child on a track in the middle of a remote island.

I wandered, awestruck by this sudden turn of events, convinced that my family would have got the ferry back to the mainland without me, and I would be left to fend for myself on this wind-battered slice of land. The world was suddenly still; nothing was being required of me; I could stand in the quiet of my own skin.

The crunch of my sandals on the grit, the keening of the gulls, the whirring of the wind in the blackthorn trees at the side of the path. Where would I sleep? What would I eat? Who would tell me when to go to bed? Then some headscarved ladies found me and fed me biscuits as they took me back to the quay, where the boat—and my family—were waiting.

Not long after that, I ran away from home. It was a move to which I had given a great deal of consideration: where I would go (a copse on a distant hill, seen from the dormer attic window), what I would take with me (books, a sandwich, the cat), how I would get money (I would steal, regrettably but necessarily). An argument over a game, a meal I didn't want, a disagreement about clothing: I forget the actual catalyst but I remember rushing to the understairs cupboard, unhooking my duffel coat from its brass peg, shoving my hands into its unyielding woollen sleeves and doing up the brown toggles, one by decisive one. This is it, I was thinking. I am leaving.

I yanked open the door, with its grainy, aquatic glass, through which I had first seen my younger sister, approaching up the front path, held in my mother's arms—a floating white ovoid, topped with fiery red, which resolved into a baby with auburn hair the closer to the house they got. I stepped through that door, letting it slam behind me with a satisfying thud, and I was off, down the path, past the twinned holly trees, with their scarlet clusters of berries and their cream-frilled leaves, through the rickety white gate and along the pavement, my legs moving under me, my buckled shoes—scuffed at the toes, always scuffed, no matter how often my mother polished them, going at their leather, punctured into patterns, with a buffer made from a cut-up corduroy jacket of my father's—clattering past the neighbours' rockeries and camper-vans and slumbering kerbside dogs.

I got as far as the crossroads, which was the perimeter of my solitary world, as far as I was allowed to go alone. We would loiter here, on occasion, for my father to come home from work if we had important news to impart: the death of a pet fish, the arrival of a visitor, the time my sister leapt off the sofa and hit her nose on the edge of the bookcase and had to go to hospital for stitches (she bears the scar to this day).

I was hesitating here, watching the cars go by, engaged with an internal debate as to whether the event of my leaving home meant I was now outside such rules as never to cross this junction, when my mother caught up with me. She had run from the house in her apron and her face was distraught. For a moment, as I saw her bearing down on me, I thought she was angry, that I was in terrible trouble. But she caught me in a close, enveloping embrace, and murmured, "Don't go, don't go," into my hair.

I will be reminded of this moment when, almost two decades later, I say goodbye to her as I'm leaving for Hong Kong. We're on the platform of the local station, I have my backpack at my feet and the branch-line train is coming through the tunnel. I'm about to get onto it and I won't be back for a long, long time. She doesn't tell me not to go but the grip of her fingers on my shoulders is the same: heartfelt, insistent, infused with the awareness that I was always going to leave, that we both knew, on some level, that the urge had always been in me.

I must, I now see, have driven her to distraction as a child: my intractability, my wildness, my irrational refusals, my craving for independence, my constant assertions of autonomy. "You were," she is given to saying these days, with a sigh, "a nightmare to rear." And I can believe it. Photographs of me show a gauche, awkward middle child, nose too large, teeth growing in crooked, a stormy yet wary expression on my face, a poorly rendered version of my prettier, more equable older sister. I was contrary. I had tantrums. I was given to screaming fits, emotional outbursts, peaks and troughs of passion. "Is she still difficult?" relatives would ask, with a wary air. They had only to spend half an hour in my company to know the answer.

"Don't provoke her," my parents would say warningly, to my sisters, and to me: "You must learn to control yourself."

I did try. I remember trying. I remember thinking that I mustn't get riled, I mustn't lose my temper, that I must above all stay in control. I would look at myself in the mirror and arrange my features into a calm smile and say the word *good-natured* to myself. I must have read it in a book. This was what I wanted to be, what I knew I ought to be. This was what nice children were: good-natured. But then I'd be told to wear a certain jumper, which was an offensive mustard colour, the neckline of which scratched and itched at my skin in an unbearable fashion and it would be boiled potatoes again for tea, and how I loathed their floury edges and their solid starchy interiors. A glass of milk would be waiting at my place-setting and I dreaded its drinking, the sinister silky coating of it as it passed down my gullet, the jaundiced swirls of cream on its surface, the pearlescent bubbles at the rim. I would be thinking all these things and then something minor, something innocuous, would happen—a comment or a look from my sister, a foot jostling against mine as I was trying to read, a page of maths homework that seemed endless and impenetrable and yawning—and there I would go. A breaking sensation somewhere in my chest, a flood of heat to the head, a sudden screech, perhaps a stamped foot. Control lost. A nature not good at all.

At the time, my mother had a particular way of expressing her frustration with me. She used to mutter, under her breath, at the dinner table, as we stood together by my wardrobe or in the bathroom or at the car door, in any situation where she and I took opposing views: "If you have easy children there's no justice in the world."

The world evidently does operate on a judicial system because my third child, a girl with untameable curls, is also an escapologist, a bolter. The minute she is released from a car or a buggy or a door, off she goes, feet barely touching ground, ringlets flying, without a backwards glance. I have countless photos of her in motion, far ahead, a speck on a narrow path, a blur on a pavement, a small person about to be swallowed by a vanishing point. "I want to go on the run," was one of her first sentences, said imploringly from the constraints of her pram.

When she was fourteen months old, realising this gene was twisted irrevocably into her double helices, I took her to the pavement outside our house.

"This," I said, pointing at the kerbstone. "You never step off this. okay? Never. This is where your feet stop."

She scanned my face with her hazel-green eyes, fascinated. "Feet," she repeated, latching on to the only word she knew.

I pointed again at the kerb. "Feet," I said, "stop."

"Feet stop."

I smiled at her and nodded. "Okay," I said, "let's give it a try."

I let go of her hand.

I narrowly avoided death on the main street of a town in the Brecon Beacons in South Wales. Was it Abergavenny, Crickhowell, Llandeilo? I forget exactly where.

It was possibly around the time I got lost in Ireland. I have a feeling I was wearing the same top, a striped nylon T-shirt with a zip I could do up with my teeth. There was a ribbon of shops along a street—a butcher, a pub, a teashop, a single petrol pump. I was waiting by the side of our car, a red Renault, under the seats of which were stashed my sister's cloth nappies, and my father was holding my hand.

It must have been blustery—were we up high in those sandstone mountains?—because I recall the sensation of my still-blond hair rustling at my cheek, over the opening of my ear.

Out of the corner of my eye, I spied my mother across the street, with my sisters. She had been into one of the shops, buying our tea or getting a treat, a tube of sweets, a packet of biscuits. And I did what I always did, what I was unable not to do. I slipped my father's grasp and I ran towards my mother and my sisters, except this time there was a road there, beneath my sandal soles.

I saw the expression on my mother's face change before I was aware of the car. I heard her scream; I heard my father yell. This set panic going within me, like the triggering of an alarm. The sense that I was somehow in trouble was filling my mind and then I heard the crunch of brakes, the shriek of tyres on tarmac, a loud shout, what was possibly a swear word.

The car was blue, with silver bumpers and rust patches. These colours imprinted themselves on my eye: the blue, the silver, the red-brown. It swerved and I swerved, and I felt the grainy chrome of the bumper whisk the back of my thigh.

I remember that I kept going. I kept moving my feet, kept powering on through the mountain air, as if nothing could touch me, nothing bad might happen, if I could just keep going, keep running, keep moving.

WHOLE BODY

1993

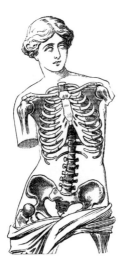

The plane is in half-darkness, engines emitting a steady hum. Everyone around me is sleeping: a woman across the aisle has two children sprawled over her lap, a couple behind me prop each other up, slack-mouthed. We are cruising somewhere over the Pacific Ocean, at that vague halfway point in a long-haul flight when your grasp on time, on personal space, on hunger has dissolved and the hours are merging and collapsing together.

The plane is full of nuns and priests, grey-garbed, beatific of face, sensibly shod. After stopping in Hong Kong, the flight will head on to Manila, and it seems to me the entire religious community of the Philippines is returning from London.

An elderly priest is seated next to me, in full white and gold robes. His spectacles slide down his nose as he sleeps. Every now and again, with exhausting frequency, he wakes me by touching my arm, indicating that he needs me to step out of my seat so he can go to the toilet. His rosary beads swing from the coat hook above us.

I sit through this night, too hot and then too cold, wondering what it is I have done, what I'm doing here, reading a battered copy of a Czech novel, pressed into my hands by a friend as we said goodbye, along with a tiny package that contained a compass because, as he wrote in the accompanying card, it was important for me "to find my way back."

I am in the wrong life, or so I think. I am off course, I am spinning in space, in more ways than one. I have left behind the life I was supposed to be leading and here I am instead, on a plane heading for Hong Kong, a city where I have no job, no prospects, and know only one person.

Crossing time zones in this way can bring upon you an unsettling, distorted clarity. Is it the altitude, the unaccustomed inactivity, the physical confinement, the lack of sleep, or a collision of all four? Travelling at speed, thousands of feet above ground, in the cabin of an aircraft, induces an altered state of mind. Things that may have been puzzling you perhaps come into focus, as if the lens of a camera has been twisted. You may find, sliding into your mind, answers to questions that have long eluded you. As you gaze out at the illusory landscape of altostratus mountains, you may catch yourself thinking: ah, of course, I hadn't realised that before.

I hold the compass in one hand, a Hong Kong map in the other—a perplexing, incomprehensible tangle of streets, elevations, tunnels, islands and harbours, with everything marked in Chinese characters. It seems to me that the act of walking away from my friend—yesterday, today, the day before?—has unloosed something within me, almost as if he has retained the end of some vital thread and my leaving means that it has been unravelling ever since, stretching out between me and all that I have left behind. How far can it extend and will it break and shall I ever be able to wind it back in?

The question comes to me slowly, creeping up on me, overtaking me and wreathing itself around me, like a fog, as the plane flies inexorably on: Why am I leaving? How come I'm going away? At university, I sat opposite this man, most days, in the library, and we revised for our finals together. We kicked each other, under the desk, gently, insistently, if our attention wandered. He would wordlessly imitate the way I shook out the muscle cramp in my hand. He made sure I didn't forget to eat lunch. When I told him I wanted to write, he didn't laugh but tilted his head in a serious, thoughtful fashion, as if letting this idea find its place in his mind.

Somehow, though, I am on this plane and I am heading towards a different man. I have, in short, no idea what I'm doing. I ought—or so it seems to me—to be moving into a flat in Cambridge. I should be oiling the chain of my bicycle. I should be going up and down the steps of the university library, carrying books and periodicals. I should be starting my PhD. I should be sitting in my usual seat, opposite my friend, who is at this very moment embarking on his own PhD, alone, without me.

Instead I am here, on my way to Hong Kong, because four months ago, I went to look for my degree results, which were displayed on a board, and instead of the result I had been hoping for, the result I needed to secure post-graduate funding, the result I had wanted and worked for, I had nothing near it. Nothing even close. Something, I realised, as I turned away from the board, as I stumbled down the steps, as I climbed back onto my bicycle, ignoring the calls from other people, had gone terribly, horribly wrong.

So here I am. I will not become an academic; I will not be staying at Cambridge; I will not see my friend for a long time. I will not be doing a PhD on the deceptively marginal roles of women in medieval poetry.

My thesis, which would have argued that the anonymous poet of *Sir Gawain and the Green Knight* was female, will remain unwritten. I have, for months now, ever since my plans caved in, caught glimpses of the poem, as if out of the corner of my eye, and have had to turn away from it because its loss from my life is too great. The celebratory meal, interrupted by the fearfully courteous giant. The poet's lingering, admiring description of his physique ("For of bak and of brest al were his bodi sturne/ Bot his wombe and his wast were worthily smale"). Her luxurious indulgence in colour and decoration, pattern and textile, the way she—I was always so sure she was a she—deftly distracts you, like a conjuror, from the central mystery with an array of handsome men and their clothes, their armour, their beards and their somewhat ridiculous fights. The intriguing and modern-seeming way she would change tense in the middle of a stanza. And the doltish Gawain, who has no idea what he's got himself into, who overlooks the old woman at the castle, entirely missing the whole point of the confusing web spun around him.

It has all gone. I must shut the door on it—and her. I liked my connection with her, through the words of the story. I relied on it. I felt as though I had reached back through time, down through the pages of the book, and taken hold of her hand. But I must give her up. I won't read the book again for many years.

At the time, as I fly across the Pacific Ocean, age twenty-one, it feels as if something crucial to my very existence—a heart, a lung, an artery—has been snatched away from me.

. . .

In a year or so, I will realise that the mess I made of my finals was nothing of the sort; in a few years more, it will seem to me that it was a merciful escape. That my guardian angel, glancing down from her cloud and seeing me cycle to my exams, perceived what might happen and let slip a celestial spanner that well and truly jammed my works.

The truth is that I would have been a terrible academic: I am too volatile, too skittish, too impatient. Once I had written my paean to the *Gawain* poet, I would have been miserable poring over ancient manuscripts in a library for the rest of my life. The opacity of Middle English would have driven me mad. I wouldn't have made a good teacher either. I'm haunted, for one thing, by a stammer: how could I have stood up at the front of a class? How could I ever have thought I could deliver a lecture? I would have been beside myself with boredom and rage and frustration within a month or two, probably left Cambridge and done something else. Maybe I would have ended up in Hong Kong anyway.

Of course I don't know this as I sit on the plane. I'm still submerged in panic and grief, still mourning the loss of what I felt was central to my identity. My grades, and my ability to produce them out of a hat, were the only thing I had, the only thing I was good at. I was not amiable or affable and never would be, I had strange and unruly hair, I was verbally challenged, I had mysterious neurological problems but, from my early teens, this was the kind of alchemy I could pull off: you were given the work, you revised the work (hard, very hard, with timetables and test papers and clocks and early starts and late nights, with notes and highlighters and index cards), then you reproduced it in an exam hall. And then—abracadabra!— you received a piece of shiny paper saying you had passed Go, you had won two hundred pounds, you had a get-out-of-jail-free card.

It had worked for years, this formula. It had taken me through two comprehensive schools (one frightening and bewildering, one less so), then on to Cambridge, through my first year and second year, and then, suddenly, in my third, final and most important year of all, the spell stopped working. It wore off.

What I wish I had known, age twenty-one, as I cycled away from the results board towards the meadow by the river in Cambridge, where I would throw stones into the water and cry, is that nobody ever asks you what degree you got. It ceases to matter the moment you leave university. That the things in life which don't go to plan are usually more important, more formative, in the long run, than the things that do.

You need to expect the unexpected, to embrace it. The best way, I am about to discover, is not always the easy way.

So, I am heading to Hong Kong. Because I have to get away. Because I don't speak any languages, besides inept German (*Ich habe alle meine Hausaufgaben gemacht*). Because Britain is in the grip of a recession and there are no jobs, especially for someone with an unremarkable degree in English literature. Because Anton, who went out to Hong Kong a while ago, has written to me and said: come, you'll easily get a job here, you can stay with me. Because this appears to be the best thing to do. Because at twenty-one, it seems a perfectly feasible plan to leave and go all the way across the world with just a rucksack and no money and the promise of a place to stay. Because why not? What else do I have to lose?

There is no warning—just a sudden clunking noise and the sensation of a cold wind flowing through the cabin.

Suddenly the plane is falling, dropping, plummeting, like a rock thrown from a cliff. The downwards velocity is astonishing, the drag, the speed of it. It feels like the world's most unpleasant fairground ride, like a dive into nothing, like being pulled by the ankles into the endless maw of the underworld. My ears and face bloom petals of pain, the seatbelt cutting into my thighs as I am thrown upwards.

Around me, the cabin is shaken like a snow globe: handbags, juice cans, apples, shoes, sweaters rise from the floor. Oxygen masks swing like lianas from the ceiling and human beings are tossed into the air. I see the child from across the aisle hit the roof, feet first, his mother arcing in the other direction, her black hair fanned out around her, her face more disgruntled than afraid. The priest next to me is thrown upwards and out of his seat, towards his rosary beads. Two nuns, their wimples billowing, are flung, like rag dolls, up to the lights.

The air is filled with screaming, with curses, with prayer. A man with blood coursing out of both nostrils starts to yell in a language I don't understand, gesticulating wildly. Drops of blood scatter from his face to mark the seats, the ceiling.

Still the plane falls. An air hostess crawls along the aisle. She is screaming, her hat askew, her hair spilling over her shoulder. Another crew member, a man, coming in the opposite direction, stumbles over her blindly. He is shouting about masks, about how we must put them on, but he is thrown upwards before anyone can hear him.

What I feel is not so much calm as numbed resignation. I think: so now this. I think: this is one of the worst things I have ever seen. I think: we are going to die, all of us, right now. We will hit the ocean or the ground at speed and we will explode like cans of soda. There will be nothing left. Total obliteration.

There is an odd relief in being alone. I glance around at people clinging to their companions, their relatives, crying, screaming, holding on tight. I grip the seat arms and tell myself, here it comes. There is no flashing of life before the eyes. No final reckoning takes place, no onslaughts of wisdom, no last-minute wishes or requests or prayers. I don't think about all the other times I have managed to hoodwink this moment, slip from its grasp. I am suffused, preoccupied, distracted by the physical, the deafening noise of the aircraft, of people's panic, the assaulting drag of the fall, the bracing of my body for the inevitable impact.

At some point, the priest must have taken my arm because when we stop falling, when the plane seems to come up against something, we are all violently thrown upwards again before finally levelling out, and I feel the clench of his fingers near my elbow, his rosary beads pressing into my flesh. In a day or two, Anton will ask me what the strange row of marks on my arm is, and I will look down and see them, a novena of bruises.

. . .

When we land in Hong Kong, most of the passengers are taken away for medical treatment, including my priest. I carry his bag for him to the door of the ambulance. When we say goodbye, he places his hand on my head and mutters a blessing in Latin. Although I am no longer a believer, although I have rejected that whole part of my upbringing, I stand there on the runway, under his hand, until it is over.

I can still feel the imprint of his fingers on the top of my head, like the circlet of an invisible crown, when I come through the gate to find Anton waiting for me. He looks different, wearing a loose white cotton shirt, his hair shorn close and dark to his scalp.

I get a job two days later, coaching school children in English literature, easing them towards good grades. I sit in a partitioned booth above the harbour and help them through *Romeo and Juliet*, through Seamus Heaney's naturalist, through the motivations of Arthur Miller's salesman. I teach a girl, who is about to be sent to a boarding school in Hertfordshire, how to use a knife and fork. She asks me to help her choose an English name and I attempt to steer her away from "Winsome" or "Delicate," which she has found in the dictionary. I take Cantonese lessons: *yat, yee, sam, sei, ng*. I eat congee every morning at a streetside stall. I swim in the South China Sea and pick up shells with my toes. I travel up the side of a peak in a slant-floored tram. I consider the newspapers, the features, the interviews, the book and film reviews, and ask myself, that? Could I maybe do that? I write letters on frail-skinned blue aerogrammes. Anton teaches me to use a single-lens-reflex camera and I go out with it and photograph everything—people taking their caged birds for a walk, old ladies doing t'ai chi in the morning, mah-jong players in the park, children dressed up as dragons, the flattened ducks in restaurant windows, the trams, the neon scribbled in the dark sky, the pyramids of durians and tanks of tofu in the night markets. I join the British Council library, scrabbling together the necessary forms and photocopies and proofs of address. I tread the carpet along the rows of Fiction A–Z and think: I can read whatever I want. The realisation arrives like a gale, lashing past me, almost making me stagger.

No more courses, no more curricula, no more exams for me.

I take out three books and, days later, I'm back, taking out three more. Books stack up in our tiny apartment, by the bed, in the bathroom, in the galley kitchen. I take out books by people I've heard of but have never had time to read, books by authors I've heard speaking on the radio, books translated from far-flung languages, books by people who are still alive, books I've seen in the pages of newspapers, all the books, in short, which didn't appear on my degree course. I read as I walk to work, I read on the underground trains, I read between my students' slots, I read in the bath, watched from the ceiling by the leucistic gecko I have tamed, plying him with aphids I pluck from the window-boxes.

And, one night, in the monsoon season, when the rain is a constant, lulling hum outside the windows, when our clothes, the windows, the pictures are growing mould in the humidity and it's too hot to sleep, when I have been reading subversive versions of European folktales, I get the urge to put down some words. I get up, find a pencil, open an exercise book at the table and, as Anton sleeps, I start to write.

NECK

2002

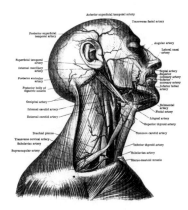

When I am seized suddenly and roughly from behind, my first thought is that it's someone I know. An acquaintance is here, in Chile, by amazing and unaccountable coincidence, and has seen us, walking beside a lake, and has come up behind us to say hello, jumping on me in a playful fashion.

Then I see Will's face and know it's nothing of the sort. There is a machete being held to my throat. Its long blade glints in the evening sun. I can feel its cool, metallic caress against my skin, the insistence of the stranger's grip, pinning my arms to my sides. In the disturbing intimacy of the embrace, his breath, laboured and hoarse, grazes my ear. Even though I can't see him, I sense that he's about my height and dark-haired. He hasn't washed for a while. I am aware of the onion-tang of his armpits, the steel of his belt-buckle in the small of my back, the tremble of his hands. He is scared, Will is scared, but I feel strangely removed, as if this isn't really happening, as if we haven't been apprehended by a machete-wielding man but are continuing with our lakeside walk.

Will is angry too, I see, at this interruption, at this

escapade. His face is white and scowling. I have known him for ten years, have been in a relationship with him for three, and I can see the whir of thought through his brain, can read it like ticker-tape coming out of a machine: a machete, my girlfriend, a man, smaller than me. He looks pissed off. He looks murderous.

We are in the first week of a long trip through South America. This little town, beside a lake, at the base of a volcano, is our second stop. After this, we plan to head for the hills, travel deep into the Andes, where we've been told there is a place with a thermal spring and a farmer who will let you sleep in his barn.

Will and I have just bought a flat in London, a red-brick end-of-terrace, with a tiny rhomboid of garden out the back. A railway line runs alongside it, trains lumbering past in obverse directions, making the walls tremble and shudder, the windowpanes rattle.

When we found it, it was semi-derelict, unused for years, the boards caving in, the Edwardian floral wallpaper slumping to the floor, the gas lamps leaking deltas of rusty red effluvia down the crumbling plaster. While we are in South America, the flat is being re-floored, rewired, revivified (or, at least, we hope so: missives from the builders are infrequent and unspecific). We will, we anticipate, return to electric lights, to floors that don't give way beneath our feet, to white walls, radiators, hot water, to opened-up fireplaces and a working oven. We have nowhere to live while this transformation takes place so, rather than finding a temporary place, we have decided to come travelling until our flat is ready. It works out cheaper, we reasoned, to live in South America than renting in London. We would take our work with us: we could write on the run and email articles back to Britain. The perfect plan.

Except that now a man is holding a machete to my neck and crooning, "*Dinaro*," into my ear. "*Dinaro*." Then, in case we don't understand: "Money."

Will doesn't move. He is standing in front of us now, his body tense and coiled.

"Give him money," I croak, the blade pressing down on my windpipe.

He still doesn't move.

"Will," I whisper, as the man gets a fistful of my hair and forces me to my knees, the machete grinding closer to my throat, "please. Give him the money."

I see Will glance at the machete, at the man, at me kneeling mutely before him, a blade held to my exposed neck, like some strange enforced marriage-proposal tableau, and I know he is still assessing whether he can tackle this situation in kind.

"Please," I say again.

I see him relent. He reaches slowly into the pocket of his jacket. I remember, irrelevantly, that back in the hostel bedroom we debated whether or not we'd need coats before we went out. Was it cold? Did it look like rain? Were there clouds in the sky? Should we take a walk by the lake before dinner? Why not?

Will holds out some notes. "Let her go," he says.

The man darts forward to snatch the money and the movement causes a sharp yank to my scalp. Through the pain, I glimpse a shock of black hair, a mouthful of stained teeth, jeans, a torn sweatshirt. He is young, younger than me, and clearly sleeping rough. What possessed us, I wonder, to take a walk in such a lonely, windy place?

The money does not please him. He stuffs it into his back pocket with a grimace.

"*Mas!*" he yells, slapping the ground with his machete blade. "*Mas!*"

He cleans us out. We had, only that day, been to the bank and changed a whole wedge of travellers' cheques: we were about to head off into the Andes and would need the cash. We had more money in our pockets and bags than we'd ever carried before, at any time in our travels. The man takes it all from us, pulling it out from the various places in which we'd stashed it. We hand it to him, in exchange for my neck, its arteries, its tendons, its muscles, its trachea, its oesophagus, for it all to remain in its current unbreached state.

He doesn't let go of my hair. He keeps it wrapped around his fist, throughout the robbery: his every twitch, his every movement causes my scalp to smart with pain. When we have no more money, when our pockets and wallets are empty, there is a suspended, triangular moment as the three of us look at each other. Me at Will, Will at the man, the man at me. What now? we are all thinking. He is holding the machete in one hand, my hair in the other; his pockets are full of our money. The wind whisks around us, pleating the surface of the lake, smashing the trees back and forth in the darkening sky.

The man pulls on my hair, forcing my head back and back. I can see only sky, scurrying clouds, the black arrows of birds. Back at the hostel, Will and I will talk about this moment and we will both say that we thought the man might want more. More violence, more abuse, more horror.

At the time, I gaze up at the sky, the birds, the fast-moving clouds, and I am thinking about the dense forest behind us, about how I do not want to be dragged in there, not at all. I do not want to see the trees closing over my head, feel the scratch and pluck of bushes against my skin, my clothes, the cold damp of the ground in there. My thoughts are very simple. They pulse through my head: let me go, let me go, not the forest, not the ground, please. I feel the beat of these thoughts. I imagine them passing through the bone of my skull, up the fibres of my hair and transmitting themselves into the man's hand. Let me go. Please. Also, know this: I will fight you. I will not go quietly. If you try to drag me away, I will battle you. I won't make it easy. I will struggle, every step of the way, with every last ounce of strength.

Into my field of vision comes his face, upside-down. He looks at me; I look back at him. He seems to be considering something, going over his options. I hold his gaze. Don't do it, I will him. Don't. Take the money and go. I cast about with my hands to find something to hold on to, a branch, a rock, in case he tries to pull me somewhere. But there is nothing, only small pebbles that slide and slip through my fingers.

He leans forward, over me. Some decision has been reached.

"Run," he hisses.

He yanks me to my feet and pushes me away from him, towards Will.

"Run!" he urges us again, pointing with his blade away

from the town, away from the hostel, away from everything. "You run!"

We sprint, wordlessly, along the edge of the lake, our breath entering and leaving our chests in sharp jags; my scalp throbs and stings, glowing with agony. I look back over my shoulder to check he isn't coming after us, with his angry grimace, his broken teeth, his unwashed hair, his machete, curved like a scimitar. I see him hurrying away over the stones, vaulting a fence, disappearing back into the scrubby vegetation.

Will pulls on my sleeve. We come to a halt and I hunch over, hands on my knees, trying to gulp down as much air as I can. I am nowhere near as fit as Will, who jogs and plays five-a-side football every week.

"Let's get out of here," he says, indicating the path back to town. "Can you run?"

Later, we sit at a table in the hostel. The owner, on hearing what happened, has scrawled on the whiteboard in reception, in large capital letters: DO NOT WALK BY THE LAKE—THERE ARE ARMED ROBBERS! She has also brought us cups of over-sweetened tea. "For the shock," she says, patting my shoulder, which makes me flinch. Something has caught up with me now: the fear that, beside the lake, had held itself in check has invaded my body. My arms are shaking. I keep looking over my shoulder. When I raise the cup to my lips, its rim rattles against my teeth.

In a few months' time, we will return to London. We will live in the rooms of the flat we have bought. The building work won't be anywhere near finished but we move in anyway. The roof no longer leaks, the eroding gas lamps will have gone but the toilet flushes with hot water, the walls click and rustle at night, and the garden is filled with rubble. We will circle each other in this flat, retreating to different rooms to work, to write. We don't know it but these will be our final months as two people.

Is there something about the experience beside the lake that pushed us forwards, made us exit one stage of life and enter the next? Did my escape from under the machete impress upon both of us the fragility, the mutability of human life? Either way, it won't be much longer until I take a pregnancy test and sit there in our newly painted flat, staring at the stick, waiting to see if some blue lines are going to rise towards me.

In the Chilean hostel, Will is feeling the need to talk about the robbery, to get the facts straight, the events in their correct order, to align my version with his. He goes over it, backwards, forwards, from this angle, from that. The way the man came up behind us, the way the wind must have snatched away the sound of his footsteps, the moment Will turned and saw a blade at my neck, how the man must have done it before, how he had clearly honed his method, how he wasn't that big, Will could have challenged him, could have got the machete away from him, he is sure he could, the way we had passed the man earlier, at the start of the walk, and Will had thought it was odd that he didn't meet our eyes, didn't respond to our nodded greeting.

This last observation makes me raise my head. "You know what?" I say. And I start to tell him something, something I'd never told anyone, something that almost happened when I was eighteen, and on a walk, alone.

ABDOMEN

2003

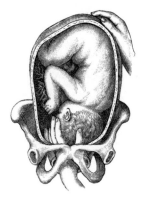

I had been distantly aware of a person to my left for some time. It was a man, nearing middle age, in hospital scrubs and mask, standing with his back against the wall of the operating theatre, just outside my field of vision. He was not taking part, but watching, just watching, his hands behind his back, like someone at a tennis match.

I had wondered, fleetingly, what he was doing there, hanging around at the fringes of an emergency Caesarean section, with apparently nothing to do. But then events overtook me and I stopped wondering about anything at all.

I still don't know who this man was and I never will. His scrubs were beige; everyone else's were blue. Was he a hospital orderly, a surgical student, a porter, a nurse? I have no idea.

What I did know, at the time of our encounter in the operating theatre, was three things: that the baby was out and somewhere over in the corner, screaming and being attended to, that I was desperate to lay eyes on him, that I was in trouble. My heart was suddenly galloping, as if trying to outrun whatever it was that was catching up with us. Will was being gripped by the arm and hustled away by a nurse. The floor was awash with blood and people were running. It is never a good sign, I've found, when medics run. On the whole, they are an unflappable, rational breed with a deliberately neutral demeanour. It's only when you see this façade slip—if they hurry or raise their voices—that you need to worry.

The doctors on the other side of a hastily erected curtain were treading red shoe-prints as they worked. One, a young woman from Northern Ireland, was panicking, saying, "I can't, I can't, I don't know how." I caught sight of a forearm, scarlet to the elbow, swiping at a sweaty brow. The other doctor, a taciturn man in his thirties, said something sharp to her, then fell silent. The anaesthetists who, until a moment ago, were sitting next to me, chatting and joking, were now standing, watching what was happening over the curtain. Their faces were still, stony, careful. One adjusted his half-moon spectacles and did something to the clear, suspended bag on a drip-stand.

Whatever it was hit my veins almost immediately and I felt myself veer sideways, like a train diverted to a different track, felt something like fog blow over my brain. My eyes rolled back in my skull—I saw the ceiling tiles, moving like a conveyor-belt, I saw the underside of the anaesthetist's chin, reddish bristles poking through the

skin, I saw a defective light flicker on and off. I forced
my eyelids to stay open; I pressed my fingernails into my
palms. I needed to remain in the here and now. I should
not give in to whatever was pulling me under. There was
a baby. I needed to stay.

When I was heavily pregnant I met an off-duty consultant
obstetrician at a party.

"The thing about childbirth," he slurred to me, in a
confidential tone, gesturing with his wine glass towards
my stomach, "is that it's either all fine or it completely
fucks up. There's nothing in between."

Not the most comforting pronouncement but perhaps
one of the most honest. When I got pregnant, I was
blithely unaware of the highly politicised arena of elective
Caesareans in the UK. I'd never heard of what was then
called the National Institute for Clinical Excellence (or
NICE, as it was known to its friends) or its strict surgical
guidelines as to how many Caesareans were permitted
per month, per hospital.

I tripped along to my appointment at a large London
hospital with a friendly registrar (who would, months
later, be the one to say, "I can't, I can't, I don't know how,"
as I was bleeding out on the operating table). I explained
to her that, as a child, I'd had a virus that meant I was

in a wheelchair for a year and left me with mild muscle, nerve, and brain damage. The neurologists and paediatricians who had looked after me said that, should I ever have children, I would need a Caesarean. I had sustained damage to the neuromuscular junctions in my spine and pelvis, which meant that labour would begin but not progress; the contractions would not be strong enough.

I wanted to ask the registrar what she thought—I would have preferred a natural childbirth and this diagnosis was, after all, twenty years old. I had rehearsed this speech, pared it back to its bare bones: I knew the registrar would be busy, that there would be long queues in the antenatal department, that I would need to get across the salient information about my childhood encephalitis and no more. All I wanted from her was her opinion: What did she think were my chances of a natural birth? But I got halfway through my speech before the registrar nervously interrupted me.

"I'll have to check this with the consultant," she said, and scurried away.

I waited. I looked around the room. I studied the lists of foods forbidden during pregnancy. I tried to read my notes upside-down.

The door flew open. A tall man with severe comb-tracks in his black hair came in, the registrar behind him. She introduced me and he took my proffered hand, but instead of shaking it, he used it to yank me bodily up out of my seat.

"Get up," were his first words to me. "Let me see you walk."

I wish now I'd left there and then, but at the time I was so astonished I complied.

"There is nothing wrong with you," he pronounced, after he'd seen me take two steps. "You will have a normal delivery."

I started to ask for clarification but the consultant—we'll call him Mr. C—talked over me. Caesareans were a cult, he said, a fashion. I had been reading too many gossip magazines. I assured him this was not the case but he shouted me down again: Did I realise that Caesareans constituted major surgery? Why had I allowed myself to be swayed by celebrities? Did I doubt his medical expertise? What was wrong with me, that I was so afraid of a bit of pain?

Angry now, I attempted to say that I was in fact quite used to pain, but he surveyed me with an expression of utmost contempt.

"This illness you claim to have had"—he turned at this point to eyeball the registrar, who was hovering by the door—"Encephalitis, was it?" The registrar nodded and

Mr. C turned his gaze back to me. "Do you have any proof?" he said, a slight but triumphant smirk curling his lips.

"Proof?" I repeated, incredulous. "You think I'm lying?"

Mr. C shrugged but continued to stare at me in a way that seemed practised, habitual. Was this his tried-and-tested method for humiliating pregnant women into submitting to his will? It seemed that way.

"Well, I suppose I could get my old hospital notes," I said, after a moment, holding his gaze. "Would that be sufficient proof for you?" You can't bully me, was the subtext of this. Mr. C saw that and it angered him further. "They'll date from the early 1980s," I continued, "and will come from South Wales, but I'm sure that can be arranged."

He narrowed his eyes, tapped his pen on the desk. And then Mr. C had had enough of me. He rose to his feet, dismissing me with a wave, and delivered his parting shot: "If you had come to me in a wheelchair, maybe then I would have given you a Caesarean."

It was an extraordinary thing to say to anyone, let alone someone who has actually been confined to a wheelchair. It wasn't Mr. C's refusal to discuss my case, never mind grant me an elective Caesarean, that horrified me, it was his implication that I was some kind of malingering coward, trying to lie my way into an easy birth. That and his appalling, patronising bullying. Did I realise that a

Caesarean was major surgery? No, I thought it was a stroll in the park.

It was only when I got outside that I started to shake, in much the same way as I had when I was in the grip of viral immobility. Ataxia is the word for it, a wavering of the limbs, a tremble, an inability to walk or coordinate. I leant up against the hospital wall, alongside the smokers, the idling ambulances, people waiting for their taxis, trying to understand, to catch up with what had just happened.

To be so unheard, so disregarded, so disbelieved: I was unprepared for this. I also felt helpless, blocked in. I wanted to run from that hospital and never go back, but how else would the baby be born? I needed this place. I was trapped, pregnant; this baby would have to come out in less than five months and what would happen if the neurologists' predictions came true? What then? What if my body was unable to birth this child? I had been foolish, selfish in getting pregnant; I should never have allowed it, if I wasn't up to the task of giving birth. What had I been thinking?

People left me alone, stepping around me. A person leaning against a wall outside a hospital, shocked and silent, is not an unusual or unlikely sight. Eventually, a man with a crutch and a drip-stand, nautical tattoos swarming up his arms, limped over and offered me a cigarette. I thanked him and shook my head, pointing to the curve of my stomach.

"Kids," he said to me genially, in a strong Cork accent. "They'll have you in an early grave."

When I got home, Will, after some initial shock at my dishevelled appearance, listened to my incoherent, rambling account of the appointment. He paced up and down the living room for a while. Then he phoned the hospital. He spoke to the Northern Irish registrar who said that, yes, I could change hospitals if I wanted to but the other options were quite a distance from where we lived. What might be better, she said, was if I stayed at the hospital but changed consultants. I wouldn't have to see or speak to Mr. C ever again, if that was what I wanted.

That was exactly and precisely what I wanted: never to see him again. So I stayed at the local hospital. I changed consultants. I scribbled out every instance of Mr. C's name from my notes with indelible ink and wrote in the new woman's name. I obliterated him from all my records, all my plans, all my folders. He was to have nothing more to do with me or my baby.

As things turned out, the predictions of the neurologists from the 1980s were right. My labour went on and on but didn't progress: my contractions surged forward, then weakened off. They felt, to me, like the apogee of pain, of agony—it was as if my body was trying to turn itself inside out—but the nurses frowned at the monitor strapped to my belly. Not strong enough, they said. Fading away, they said.

I kept trying to explain; Will kept trying to explain. The thing is, I said, addressing a midwife whom Will had grabbed by the arm, I had acute encephalitis as a child. Severe cerebellar ataxia. Neurological damage. Vestibular malfunction. Please check my birth-plan, my notes. It's all in there. My neuromuscular junctions are—here, I yanked the gas-and-air mask off my face—they are . . . they are . . . faulty and they said I'd need a . . . a . . . Wait, wait, where are you going? Come back.

On the morning of my third day in labour, who should appear at my bedside but Mr. C. I looked up at him from the bed; he looked back, his lip curled. Did he remember me from our meeting all those months ago? Had he seen the traces of his name scored out of my notes? I wanted to shout, not you, anyone but you, but I knew, in some shape or form, that my baby's life was in his hands, my life was in his hands. He was the only consultant on duty that morning: there was no other. So I was polite, I was controlled; I didn't shout, I didn't ask him to leave. I may have even smiled as I begged him for a Caesarean, from my prone position on a bed, getting out the words between contractions.

He glanced at the charts of my baby's dipping heart-rate, read over my notes, perused my birth-plan, then granted me surgery, in the manner of a landowner bestowing a favour on a serf. But Mr. C still had me down as a hysteric, a fantasist, a malingerer, a reader of celebrity gossip. It would, he said, go down in my records as "by maternal request"—that is, medically unnecessary. This, despite three days of labour, the induction drugs, the non-progression, the diagnosis by neurologists.

The next day, after my messed-up C-section, the surgeon came to visit, to see how I was, to explain what had gone wrong. The problem, he told me, as I sat up in bed, attempting to breastfeed, had been that the baby had become wedged in what is termed "star-gazer presentation," a position that makes natural delivery impossible. My labour had been allowed to go on for so long, without progressing, that the baby had turned the wrong way, his spine aligning with mine, and because my cervix hadn't dilated, his chin was forced down and the widest part of his head was facing the exit. Head down, looking up. Some of us are looking at the stars. His left ear was so crushed and misshapen by the pressure of the contractions-that-went-nowhere that it would require plastic surgery.

The baby's wedged and immovable position made it difficult for the surgeons to remove him and, somehow, in the ensuing wrestling and grappling, clutching and heaving, something had ruptured. All that should have stayed inside had come out.

"What would have happened," I asked the surgeon, the man who had replaced my intestines and stopped my bleeding, sewn me up and saved my life, "a hundred years ago, if you had a star-gazer baby?"

The surgeon looked up from his notes. He seemed to be considering the question, debating whether or not to tell me the truth. "You wouldn't have made it," he said eventually, going back to whatever it was he was writing.

"What about the baby?"

"The baby would have died first," he said, not looking up. "Then the mother. Of sepsis. Probably days later."

Death by childbirth seems such an outdated danger, such a distant threat, particularly in the surroundings of hospitals in the developed world. But a recent survey* ranked the UK at 30 out of 179 countries for maternal health. In the UK, a woman faces a one in 6,900 chance of dying in childbirth, which far exceeds the risk in Poland

* Save the Children's annual State of the World's Mothers Report for 2015.

I AM, I AM, I AM

(19,800), Austria (19,200) or Belarus (45,200). The US ranked lower than the UK, at 33, with a woman facing a one in 1,800 chance of maternal death. At 179 is Somalia. All but two of the eleven lowest-ranking countries in the world are in West and Central Africa.

The most common cause of maternal mortality worldwide is postpartum haemorrhage.

When I was a child, we were taken every Christmas to see a pantomime. I found these to be disturbing, hectic events: men in dresses, with balloon breasts, shouting like maniacs, children from the audience taken up on stage to stand there, tongue-tied and blinking, adults dressed as rabbits and hedgehogs hurling boiled sweets into the auditorium, heavy velvet curtains with gold frogging and then—most disquieting of all—a thick, flesh-coloured blind dropping down, emblazoned with the harrowing words FIRE CURTAIN.

I remember seeing a man shut a spangle-leotarded woman inside a box, her feather-adorned head protruding at one end and her tiny slippered feet at the other. He then proceeded to slice the box in half, the serrated teeth of the saw hacking and grinding as they slid further and further through the beautiful, gaudy girl.

What horrified me most, as a child, was that she smiled

the whole time, her teeth bared towards us, lips drawn back, even when the man swung open the box to show us the severed vacancy that he—mad man, murderer, psychotic—had created while we just sat in our seats and gawped, inert as argon.

The leotard woman flashes through my mind as I lie there on the operating table, sliced open, ruptured, bleeding, my intestinal tract unravelled, on the wrong side of my skin. Whatever it is the surgeons are doing to me on the other side of the curtain is rough, violent, violating. I am not smiling. I am not wiggling my sequinned toes. I am being shunted up the table, bit by bit, until my head rests on the metal edge. I can feel hands rummaging through my innards, as far up as my ribs. Still the blood comes. I catch my first glimpse of the baby, my son, far away across the room, and his face is uncertain, anxious, his brow furrowed, as if he is not sure he likes what he sees (it is an expression I will catch on his face sometimes, even as a teenager). I say something like, bring him here, and he turns his eyes towards me, as if my voice is the only familiar thing for him in the room.

We have agreed, Will and I, that he will stay with the baby in any eventuality. Don't let it out of your sight, I have exhorted him, late at night, when I have been worrying about the birth, about hospitals in general. I have read too many novels and watched too many films about babies swapped at birth, babies who weren't issued with an identity bracelet.

My grandmother used to tell the story of how she was brought a baby to feed in hospital, and she knew it wasn't hers. Of course it's yours, the nurse had replied. But my grandmother was no pushover: she rose from her bed and went down the ward, checking each cubicle, until she'd located her baby, my future aunt, who had been given to another woman. Whatever happens, I'd said to Will, over and over again, you stay with the baby at all times.

He is keeping his promise. The problem is that I can't see them any more. They seem to have been taken elsewhere, behind a screen or into another room. I am given more of whatever is in the drip and my head is hanging off the end of the table. I raise my hand. I'm not sure, now, what for. To call a halt? To say, enough? To say, help me, please?

Either way, what happens next is that the man in beige is suddenly there. He has stepped towards me, away from his wall, and he takes my raised hand. He enfolds it in both of his. I gaze up at him mutely. I had not known, until that moment, what a lonely experience it is to be in danger, in the middle of a room full of people who are frantically working to save your life. I am not prone to loneliness—I have always been someone who leans

towards solitude—but my overwhelming sensation had
been, until that moment, loneliness, isolation, bafflement.
I was slipping away, alone, surrounded by people.

The man is wearing those spectacles that react to light
so his eyes are hidden behind brown-tinted lenses. He has
thick, wiry hair cut close to his head. More hair sprouts
over the top of his surgical scrubs. He moves my hand so
that it is curled around his wrist, and he places his other
hand on top of it. His touch is infinitely gentle but firm
and sure. There is no way he is letting go, he is telling me,
entirely without words. He is going to stay right here and
I am going to stay right here. I clutch at him with the force
of a drowning woman. He nods, once, down at me and a
grave, slow smile lifts above the edges of his surgical mask.

I wonder sometimes if I imagined him, if he was the
figment of a panicking, threatened mind. He wasn't,
though. He was there, he was real.

Our interaction was entirely wordless. I don't even know
if he spoke English. He stayed with me while they stitched
and stapled me together again; he took the weight of my
head and shoulders as they lifted me from the operating
table onto a gurney. He was there when they pushed me
into a ward.

After that I lost sight of him. I was suddenly surrounded
by nurses who were swabbing me down, rearranging

drip-stands, asking about drugs, painkillers, transfusions. Someone brought in the baby.

Did the man see me reunited with my son? I hope so. When he took my hand he taught me something about the value of touch, the communicative power of the human hand. I didn't know, as I lay there, that I would think of him many times in the years ahead. When my son lay on a hospital bed, age four, with the raging fever of meningitis, I reached through the bodies of the attending doctors and held his slack, heated hand in both of mine. When my youngest child disappeared beneath the waves of the Mediterranean Sea and I had to leap in, haul her out, turn her upside-down so that the water drained from her lungs. Then all she and I could do was sit on the sand, wrapped in towels, contemplating what had almost happened, her small fingers wrapped in mine. When my middle child had eczema so torturous it made her scream and writhe through the night, I would press my hands over hers to stop the scratching, to ease her back towards sleep.

The people who teach us something retain a particularly vivid place in our memories. I'd been a parent for about ten minutes when I met the man, but he taught me, with a small gesture, one of the most important things about the job: kindness, intuition, touch, and that sometimes you don't even need words.

BABY AND BLOODSTREAM

2005

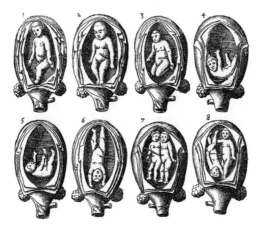

"It was nothing you did," the nurse says. "It's not your fault."

I am silent. I had not thought it might be. I look again at the image of the baby on the screen. There it is. Sitting up in its dark cave, as if waiting for something, as if on best behaviour.

If I sit straight, it seems to be saying, no one will notice.

I know how it should be, how it should look: this is, after all, my second pregnancy. I know the heartbeat should be there, flashing and flashing like a siren. So when the radiologist says that he's sorry, the baby is dead, I already know. But I carry on staring at the monitor because there is some frail, furled part of me that is hoping there has been a mistake, that the heartbeat might suddenly appear, that the scanning machine might roll further and there it will be.

I can't look away from the screen, even when the radiologist starts talking again, even when they say I can get down from the bed and get dressed. I want to burn the image of that tiny, ghost-pale form into my retina. I want to remember it, to honour its existence, however short.

We are shown into a room. It is down a corridor and around a corner, away from the antenatal department, away from all the other women waiting for their scans.

This room has curtains. The chairs have cushions. There is a large, leather-covered book on a table and a sign above it says "Book of Remembrance."

"The bad-news room," Will mutters, as he stares out of the window, as he examines the charts on the wall. And I nod. I cannot stop crying, which is odd because I usually can, if I need to. I perch on the edge of a chair and tell myself I have to stop, I have to get myself under control, but I can't. Will hands me a cushion, for some reason, and I take it. I hold it carefully, conscientiously, on my knee. It was nothing you did.

The nurse comes in. She makes a show of shutting the door very gently, as if the noise might be too much for us.

"It's what we call a missed miscarriage," she says, "where the foetus has died but not come away."

I nod again, several times, because I am still unable to speak. I think about how the phrase *missed miscarriage* must be hard to say. I wonder if the nurse has had to practise to say it so smoothly. It's the kind of sound-pattern that would trip up a stammerer: those clusters of double consonants, the repeated *i* sound. I experience a transient, irrational relief that I never became an antenatal nurse, that I never went down that particular career path. Imagine the horror of stammering as you gave someone this news, of being suddenly unable to get out the words. I almost mention this to the nurse, almost compliment her on how well she pronounced the phrase, how seamlessly she said it. I arrive at the decision, just in time, that this probably isn't appropriate.

She tells me I have three options. I can have a surgical removal, under general anaesthetic, I can go home and wait to see if things start naturally—

"That," I say, lifting my head. "I'll do that."

Around one in five pregnancies ends in miscarriage; up to 75 per cent of these occur in the first trimester.* The risk of pregnancy loss, then, in the first twelve weeks is 15 per cent. One in a hundred women experience recurrent miscarriages; a third of women in the UK attending specialist clinics as a result of miscarriage are clinically depressed.

We all, I think, know these statistics, or at least have

* Miscarriage statistics, Tommy's, tommys.org

a vague sense of them. We know miscarriage is out there, at our backs, pursuing us, like Andrew Marvell's wingéd chariot.

It's why you're not supposed to tell people you're pregnant until you've passed the magic twelve-week point, until you come out of hospital clutching a monochrome sonogram picture. Only then can you inform your friends, your in-laws, your employers; only then can you go out and buy wire-less bras and stretchy tops; only then can you leave your antenatal vitamin bottles lying about the house with impunity; only then will you start getting calls from relatives, suggesting old family names, insisting that the daily drinking of Guinness is crucial for breast-feeding, offering knitted matinee jackets, stiff with age.

I've never understood the blanket secrecy you're supposed to apply to early pregnancy. Certainly, I've never felt the need to broadcast the news far and wide, but it seems to me that pregnancy at any stage is significant, life-changing enough to warrant telling those closest to you. Even if something as devastating as pregnancy-loss happens, wouldn't you want your close friends, your family to know? Who else would you turn to at such a time? How else do you explain the grief, the stunned pain on your face, the tears, the shock?

Because losing a baby, a foetus, an embryo, a child, a

life, even at a very early stage, is a shock like no other. Intellectually, you know it's a possibility: as soon as you get the line on a test stick, you look every day for the tell-tale sign of blood, you tell yourself it might happen, you tell yourself not to build things up, not to expect too much, to be sensible, rational, balanced. But you have never had a talent for those things and, besides, your biology, your body is singing a different song, a distracting, absorbing, joyous tune: your blood capacity rises, pulsing along your veins, your breasts swell, like dough, out of your bras, the muscle and capacity of your heart increases, your appetite hears the call, responds to demand, and you find yourself in the kitchen at midnight, contemplating crackers and fish paste, grapefruit and halloumi.

Your imagination keeps pace with your teeming body: you picture a girl, a boy, perhaps twins, because there are numerous twins in your family, both identical and fraternal—your own father is one. It will be blond, it will be dark, auburn, curly-haired. It will be tall, it will be petite. It will look like its father, you, its brother, a melange of all three. It will love painting, pole-vaulting, trains, cats, puddles, sandboxes, bikes, sticks, the building of towers. You will take it swimming, you will rake leaves and light bonfires, you will push it along the seafront, you will tuck it into the basket its brother used. You tell yourself not to be stupid enough to buy anything, but then you pass, in a shop, a knitted rabbit in soft blue wool, with a yellow ribbon and a startled, quizzical expression. You reverse, you hesitate, you pick it up. Quick, while no one is looking. You picture yourself placing this rabbit inside a hospital crib, for the child to look at. Of course you take it to the till and you hand over the money, hurriedly, furtively. You carry it home, you wrap it in tissue and you hide it at the bottom of a drawer. When you are alone, you take it out and look at it.

You leaf through name books and think: Sylvie, Astrid, Lachlan, Isaac, Rafael? Who will it be? Who will be coming?

When it happens—and it will happen to you, over the years, several times—the impact is like that of a wrecking ball. Each time you lie on the scanning couch, you will stare fixedly at the faces of the radiologists as they examine the image on the screen and you will learn to recognise the expression—a slight falling, a frown, a certain freighted hesitation—and you will know before they say anything that this one hasn't made it either.

It will be hard, every time, not to listen to the internal accusations of incompetency. Your body has failed at this most natural of functions; you can't even keep a foetus alive; you are useless; you are deficient as a mother, before you even were a mother.

Don't listen to those bad fairies, you try to tell yourself. It was nothing you did.

For some reason, your body doesn't follow the normal procedure (it fails even at this, the malicious whispers say—you can't even miscarry a miscarriage). Your system doesn't get the memo that it's all over. Your hormones hurtle on. So, for you, there is never any blood, never any sign of foetal expiration at all. You find out only at a scan. You will walk around, feeling pregnant, looking pregnant, to all intents and purposes still pregnant, but the baby is dead. Sometimes your physiological inability to process the death of the foetus infuriates you, devastates you; at others it seems only apt, sane. Why give up, your body is saying, why let go, why accept this end?

So, after the terrible moment in the dark of the scanning room, you are always taken somewhere else, where you must wait for someone to come and speak with you about "what happens next." Sometimes this is a reasonable place, like the bad-news room; at other times, not. Once, you are made to wait back where all the other women are queuing for their scans and they regard you, appalled and petrified, as you sit there with your teeth gritted, your hands clamped over your face. They are too scared to sit next to you, as if what you have is catching, so you are stranded alone on an entire bank of plastic chairs. On another occasion, you are shown into what you immediately realise is a labour suite: the bed is still rumpled, there are flecks of blood on the walls; the air is filled with the screams and exhortations, then the sudden new cries of birth. You sit there, disbelieving, listening to someone in the next-door room approach the climax of labour. You send an unhinged text message to your friend: *No heartbeat,* you write, *and I'm being made to wait in, guess what, a labour suite.* She texts back: *Leave that room, walk out, I'm coming to get you.*

You do walk out. The nurse tries to stop you but you don't listen. You've been through this enough times to be fully aware of "what happens next." As you take the stairs down, away from the scanning department, you feel the notion, the idea of the child leaving you with each step. You feel its fingers loosening, disentangling themselves from yours. You sense its corporeality disintegrating, becoming mist. Gone is the child with blond or dark or auburn hair; gone is the person they might have been, the children they themselves might have had. Gone is that particular coded mix of your and your husband's genes. Gone is the little brother or sister you pictured for your son. Gone is the knitted rabbit, wrapped and ready in tissue paper, pushed to the back of a cupboard, because you cannot bring yourself to throw it out or give it away.

Gone are your plans for and expectations of the next year of your life. Instead of a baby, there will be no baby.

You must adjust to this new picture. You must give it all up. You must somehow get past the due date: you will dread its coming. On that day you will feel the emptiness of your body, your arms, your house. You must intercept the letters from the maternity unit that keep on coming, despite everything. You must pick them up off the mat, almost persuading yourself that you haven't seen them, you don't know what they are. You tear them into flitters and drop them into the bin.

You will watch your body backtrack, go into reverse, unpicking its work: the sickness recedes, your breasts shrink back, your abdomen flattens, your appetite disappears.

You will have the general anaesthetic, on the first occasion, and the foetus is removed from you while you are unconscious. After that, whenever it happens again, you admit yourself to hospital, take the drugs to induce expulsion, refuse painkillers, because somehow you want the pain, the discomfort, the ache, the searing cramps: it seems important to go through this, to experience these endings, these cleavings. Each time, you will insist on having the body of the foetus, on being able to take it home. This always seems to cause consternation, wherever you are, whichever city you are in. One doctor says you can't have it because he "needs it."

You stare at him for a moment, wondering, did he really say that or was it my imagination? "I need it," you say.

"No, you don't," says the doctor, shaking his head.

"But it's mine," you mutter, with rising menace, curling your hands into fists.

Your sister, who has stayed with you throughout this whole long day, who knows what might happen next ("don't provoke her"), gets up from her chair and steps into the corridor with the doctor. You don't know what she says to him but she returns with a small, sad, wrapped package and hands it to you.

There is a school of thought out there that expects women to get over a miscarriage as if nothing has happened, to metabolise it quickly and get on with life. It's just like a bad period, a friend of mine was told, briskly, by her mother-in-law.

To this, I say: Why? Why should we carry on as if it's nothing out of the ordinary? It is not ordinary to conceive a life and then to lose it; it's very far from ordinary. These passings should be marked, should be respected, should be given their due. It's a life, however small, however germinal. It's a collection of cells, from you and, in most cases, from someone you love. Yes, of course worse things happen every day; no one in their right mind would deny that. But to dismiss a miscarriage as nothing, as something you need to take on the chin and carry on, is to do a disservice to ourselves, to our living children, to those nascent beings that lived only within us, to the person we imagined throughout the short pregnancy, to those ghost children we still carry in our minds, the ones who didn't make it.

During the very week in which a miscarried baby of mine would have been born, I found the following passage in Hilary Mantel's memoir, *Giving Up the Ghost*:

> [Children's] lives start long before birth, long before conception, and if they are aborted or miscarried or simply fail to materialise at all, they become ghosts in our lives . . . The unborn, whether they're named or not, whether or not they're acknowledged, have a way of insisting: a way of making their presence felt.

If asked, I could reel off exactly, instantly and without hesitation, what age all my miscarried children would be, had they lived. Is this odd? Is it macabre? I have no idea. This is information I hold very close. No one has ever asked me this question and probably never will—miscarriage is still a taboo subject, one women will rarely broach, share or discuss. I can count on one hand the conversations I've had with friends about it, which is odd, if you consider how prevalent it is.

Why don't we talk about it more? Because it's too visceral, too private, too interior. These are people, spirits, wraiths, who never breathed air, never saw light. So invisible, so evanescent are they that our language doesn't even have a word for them.

On the first occasion—when I don't even know, can't even conceive that there will be more—I leave the bad-news room. I go home. I stop on the way back to buy painkillers: the nurse said I might need them. I also have to buy maternity pads and it comes to me, as Will and I drift up and down the aisles of a vast chemist in an out-of-town shopping complex, that they will be in what is called the Mother & Baby section.

I come to a stop beside a display of false eyelashes.

"What?" Will says, taking my hand. "Are you okay?"

I tell him, in as few words as possible, about the Mother & Baby section. I point it out. It is signposted by a picture of a crawling, nappied infant, turning around to smile at the camera.

We leave the false eyelashes and head across the tiled floor. I don't see, I don't look at, the sleepsuits for newborns, the nappies, the jars and jars of baby food, the barrier creams, the pillowy rolls of cotton wool, the breast pads, the boxes of formula, the bottles, the sterilisers for microwave and hob, special offer, the woman with a tiny pod-being in a sling. I don't see them, I don't. I tell myself this.

My son is lining up cars on the narrow windowsill when I get back.

"Hello," I say.

He doesn't look up from his game but he smiles to himself and whispers, "Mama." He's not big on hellos or goodbyes. "A parky base," he says instead, meaning "parking space." He slots a car between two others.

"That's great," I say. I look at him. I stare. I can't look away. The groove at the back of his neck, the dents over his knuckles, the way the hair grows in a swirl on his crown. He seems miraculous.

"Where go?" he asks, fixing me with a firm, toddler gaze.

"The hospital," I say, "but I'm back now."

He still looks at me, unblinking, a yellow car in one hand. But he doesn't ask anything else.

I go into the bedroom and pull all the maternity clothes out of my wardrobe and on to the floor. I strip off the clothes I am wearing and add them to the pile. I try to sort them, to fold them, to put tops together, then trousers, but somehow I'm crying again and shivering because the bedroom is cold. Everything is tangled: jumper sleeves cling to skirt hems, trousers are inside out, bras clutch with their hooks to T-shirts. I hurl the lot across the room, towards the wall.

Will steps through the doorway. He is in the middle of saying something but stops.

"Can you please," I shriek, and it's the first time I've raised my voice all day, and it feels surprisingly good, "get a box and put all this into it?"

He walks around the bed and surveys the scattered clothing. "What is it?" he asks.

"It's my maternity clothes. I want them put away."

I move about the house, collecting anything to do with babies. There is some stretchmark ointment in the bathroom, a row of books on the shelf, a bottle of folic-acid tablets; there are the envelopes from the hospital detailing appointments, due dates; there are cards from friends with pictures of things like prams and storks and bootees. I put all these into the box that Will has left beside the bed. I crush the lid shut. I tape it down.

Are you still pregnant if the baby is dead? I'm asking myself this as I push my son in a swing. It is a cold day.

I have dressed him in mittens, a hat, matching scarf, thick socks, wellies. He swoops towards me, then drops away, towards me, away. A stream of whitened breath streaks from his mouth.

Does it still count? There is a baby inside you, I say to myself, but it's dead. It's still in there. I imagine it clinging to the sides, those stretchy velvet walls, by its fingertips, refusing to let go. I want it out, more than anything. More than anything, I want it to stay.

A woman slides a child, older than mine, into the swing next to us. She gives me a smile and I smile back. She straightens up and I see the distended curve of her belly, the way the clothes stretch and pull over it. Eight months gone, easily, maybe nearer nine. In a month, she'll have a baby, it will be out of her and breathing.

She stands on the opposite side of the swing, and it's only as she starts to push that I notice she has more children, twins, in a double buggy behind her, and when I see this, when I see I am surrounded by children, all hers, I experience such a flash of hatred for her that I have to turn away, ashamed.

"What do you think we should do with it?" I ask Will that evening.

He is lying on the sofa, reading a paper, and makes a

"Hmm?" noise but doesn't stop reading so I come and stand in front of him.

"I don't know what to do with it," I say, "when it comes out. Whenever that may be."

He looks up.

"I don't want to bury it as we're not going to live here much longer. I mean, imagine leaving it behind here, in this city, in the garden of this flat, while we all go somewhere else. I don't want to do that, not at all. It seems an awful idea. I could never do that." I'm talking very fast but I don't seem to be able to stop. "So I don't know what to do. What do you think?"

Will is still looking at me. The paper is getting crushed in his hands. "Um," he says.

"I looked on the internet," I say. "They have all these support-group things, chat rooms, you know, for people who have . . . people who . . . people in our position."

"Really?"

"Uh-huh."

I haven't told Will that, after he goes to sleep, I'm spending a lot of time in these shadowy, unreal, half-lit places, where strangers tap out their innermost anguish in strange abbreviations: the Morse code of the miserable. "GTH" means "gone to heaven," an assumption that makes me grimace. "DD" is "dear daughter"; "DP," "dear partner." You can send virtual hugs by writing the person's name surrounded by repeating parentheses—the more there are, the more intense the gesture. You can sign your name with a list of how many miscarriages you've had and at how many weeks. There are saccharine animations of babies gaining sparkly wings and ascending up the screen. I never post anything and the whole thing makes me horribly uncomfortable, but, nonetheless, I'm fascinated, unable to look away, meting out the dark, sleepless hours of the night by scrolling through the private pain of people I don't know and will never meet.

"Anyway," I say, "someone mixed the ashes with soil in a pot, then planted a flower on top of it."

Will puts the paper to one side, frowning, rubbing at his forehead.

"I don't fancy that," I say eventually. "Do you?"

He seems unable to formulate a reply, unable to contribute to this conversation, so I turn away and pick up the phone, take it into the cupboard where the washing-machine is shushing and, sitting in the dark, I dial my friend's number.

"I don't know what to do with it," I say, "after it comes out."

I can hear her thinking. She's a medic. She studied for

I AM, I AM, I AM

twice as long as I did. She has letters after her name. She saves lives every day. She knows things.

"You need to have the operation," she says, in a modulated, level voice. I wonder if this is the one she uses to talk to her patients, to tell them unfortunate test results or frightening news. "It's a very straightforward procedure. You'll be under a general anaesthetic and when you wake up it will all be over. Phone them tomorrow and tell them. Book yourself in."

"Can't do that," I say.

The washing-machine sloshes and whirls the clothes. I see a sleeve of my son's favourite shirt reach out towards a hem of a nightgown.

"How long are you going to leave it?" she asks instead. "This isn't doing you any good, all this waiting around. Not to mention it's dangerous. They shouldn't," she mutters, almost to herself, "be letting you walk about like this."

"Dangerous?" I repeat, my voice rising. "How can it be dangerous? The baby's dead, what more can possibly—"

"I meant dangerous for you."

"For me?"

"Yes. Didn't they tell you that?"

I open the door a crack and look towards my son's bedroom. The doorway is dark, silent. "No, they didn't,"

I say, keeping the door ajar with my foot, my eye on the softly dim space where my son is lying. "Why?"

"There's a risk of infection from carrying this for days on end. An ever-increasing risk, as time goes on. Think about it logically. It's unusual, how long your body has held on to it—"

"Is it?"

She sighs. "I don't know why this has happened. Why the baby didn't make it, why your body isn't expelling it, why it isn't letting go, but these things just happen sometimes. In unusual cases. You'll probably never find out the reason. But what you need to do now is put your safety first."

I push the door away from me with the toe of my slipper and let it swing back, away, back. I don't answer but fiddle with the arrangement of washing powders on the shelf, looking again for my son's shirt in the tumbling wash.

She speaks again in her soft voice: "If it's not out in two days I'm booking you in myself."

We go to the beach. The sea is flat silver under a lapis sky. There is a single cloud near the horizon, a teasel of white. My son zooms around the sand in circles, a bucket in one hand and a piece of wood in the other. The winter sun is low and forces me to shade my eyes with my hand.

I kneel with my back to the glare and start to dig a hole for my son. He likes holes. He moves about the sand around me, always near me, as if tethered, like a small tugboat.

I dig. Water is seeping through the knees of my trousers. The plastic spade starts to bend, but I buttress it with my fingers. I hear, somewhere behind me, the shrill of Will's mobile phone and him saying, "Yeah? How are you?" and my son, also behind me, muttering something to himself. I dig, deeper and deeper, until I reach the level of water and what I am bringing up on my spade now is the consistency of new cement. I slop it on to the pile of sand beside me and what is in my mind, what I am thinking is: feather.

Most of all, it looked like a feather. Curled like that and grey-white and floating. And as I think the word "feather," the two eliding syllables of it, the susurration of its sound, my son appears at my elbow and, held in his hand, is a feather.

I hold the spade, poised above the hole. I stare at him. "What this?" he says.

I look at it. It is white, its gossamer fronds tremble in the breeze, and it is held in the grip of his thumb and finger. I clear my throat.

"It's a feather," I say and, as I do, I look for Will. Come here, I want to say. Do you know what happened? But he is over by the promenade wall, his phone clamped to his ear; he is kicking at some seaweed and speaking in bursts.

"Fevver," my son repeats, in the way he does when he hears a new word, "fevver, fevver."

"Yes," I say, "feather. From a bird. Do you know that when they fly—"

But he isn't interested in that. "For you," he says, and I take it, the feather, I cradle it in my palm.

I manage to get out a single word: "Thanks."

My son is decisive now, business-like. He points. "Sea," he says, and tugs at my hand.

We walk towards the water, where waves rise and collapse on a sheen of sand. My son is transfixed by the prints his wellies are making. I cup the feather in both hands. I think I'm about to cry but I don't.

I hold the feather high, above my head, and my son raises his face to see. I let it drop, releasing it into the air. I think it might swirl and swoop down, that he might like that, that he might pick it up and say, again, again. But it doesn't. It rises higher and higher, borne on what seems like nothing. We watch it together. Up and up and up it sails, directly over our heads, and then it vanishes.

I look back at him, at his face tilted towards the sky, at his body bundled inside his red coat.

"Gone," he says.

I nod. I take his hand. We begin the walk back up the beach and I see that Will is coming towards us now, waving and waving, as if I can't see him, as if I am far in the distance on a dark, crowded plain.

LUNGS

2000

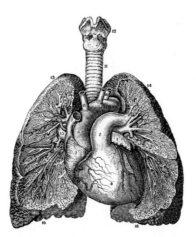

I am in the shallows of the Indian Ocean, out beyond the breakers, my shoulders and head above the surface. It is my favourite place in the sea, just before the tipping point, the releasing, chaotic thunder of the turning waves, and close enough to shore to view the land from the water.

I have lived a great deal of my life near the sea: I feel its pull, its absence, if I don't visit it at regular intervals, if I don't walk beside it, immerse myself in it, breathe its air. I take excursions to the coasts near London—the tea-coloured waves of Suffolk, the flat, silty sands of Essex, the pebbly inclines of Sussex. I have, ever since childhood, swum in it as often as I can, even in the coldest water.

There is, I find, great solace to be had from it. Karen Blixen wrote, in her *Seven Gothic Tales*, "I know a cure for everything: salt water . . . in one way or the other. Sweat, or tears, or the salt sea."

When I was a child, one of my favourite picture-books was about a childless couple living in a fisherman's cottage in the Outer Hebrides. The man finds a baby washed up on the seashore and takes it home to his wife. They know it's a selkie, a creature that slips between human and seal form, and they do everything they can to keep the boy from the sea, to trap him in his human form. To no avail, of course.

I spent hours lying on the floor of my bedroom, poring over its watercolour illustrations of cliffs, of waves, of storms and, in particular, the page where the boy dives into the sea and turns back into a seal. There was something about the duality of the selkie, a shape-shifter with two existences, a child who hankers for a different form—found in both Irish and Scottish mythology—that caught my imagination. I would, whenever I could, leap into the sea, duck my head into the water and wait for the metamorphosis, for my limbs to shrink, for my hair to disappear, for my sealskin to cover me. I would resurface crestfallen, disappointed, still in my stubbornly human form.

The watercolour pages of my selkie book flit through my mind as I tread water in the Indian Ocean. The idea of transformation, transubstantiation, still holds its lure. This water is green, marbled with white. It flexes beneath me, warm and supple. It snatches and grumbles over pebbles nearer the beach. I have a view of jagged umber cliffs, a line of woven huts, towering, yellow-topped trees. I can see a line of goats making their plaintive, clinking way down a track, a group of women stepping into the sea, sinking into it, their saris billowing around them into bright, gilded parachutes. Their laughter bounces towards me, across the water. Further down the shore, two men scrub at an elephant with brooms, the enormous creature submitting blissfully to this treatment, eyes closed, wavelets advancing and retreating around its massive, bent knees.

I rise and fall with the pulse of the sea. I wait, treading water between ocean and surf, letting the humpback of a wave approach, lift and release me, passing on. I lie back, looking up at the merciless, cloudless sky, thinking that I should maybe go in, thinking about where to visit next, thinking about the yoga class I took the day before, on the clifftop at dusk, the mellifluous voice of the instructor who, when we were bent double, gazing at our ankle bones, our arms wrapped backwards about our sacrums, reassured us that "everything is normal."

I am aware, first, of being pulled sideways, as if on a sleeper train. The current is drawing into itself, gathering together, with abrupt and decisive force. I right myself in time to see the beach pulling away from me, like disappearing theatre scenery. At this point, I don't worry too much. The sea is unpredictable—I know this. It will be fine, won't it? This is a riptide, I tell myself, a narrow gully of current, pulling out to sea. I've never been in one but have heard about them. I even drew a diagram of their workings, once, in a distant geography lesson, with different-coloured pencils to highlight the opposing directions of water.

I see Will lying on a towel, his book propped open. I see the ladies in their saris. I see the elephant, standing now, trumpeting water into the air, spattering its striated sides, the two minders, their brooms. All reeling away from me, faster than I'd ever imagined possible. I'm swimming to the best of my strength but I'm far out from the shore now, travelling fast, and my strokes are ineffectual. It's as if something or someone is holding me back by the bikini strap, halting my progress, sneering at my attempts to escape.

It comes back to me that to escape a riptide, one must swim parallel to the shore. All right, then. I turn myself ninety degrees and, at the same time, there is a rushing sound, like that of rain on a tin roof. I turn. Behind me is a wall of water, a wave larger than any I have ever seen, its top just tipping over, cresting white. I don't even have time to cry out, to shout, to call for help. I see it and, a split second later, I'm in it. It crashes over me, it seizes me, it shoves me under. I'm caught, like a doll, like a puppet, in its muscle, in the eye of its storm. I feel myself pushed down by the back of my neck and I remember a swimming teacher at school demanding that I dive, leap off the edge of the pool, split the surface of the water with the top of my skull. I wanted to but found I could not. I vacillated there, hands clenched, feet clinging to wet tile, the teacher pushing down on the back of my neck. I can't, I said, from under his hand, and the teacher frowned at me and said, there's no such word as can't, and I remember being floored, baffled by the stupidity of this reply. No such word? Of course there was. It was a contraction of two words, sure, but still a word: everybody knew that.

The wave turns me over, like an acrobat, like St. Catherine in her wheel. I feel my feet lift, feel my body invert, my head pooling with heat and pressure. There is a sharp blow to the side of my face and my eyes, shut tight against the salt, streak with technicolour, my teeth snapping together over my tongue. The noise inside a riptide is astonishing, a rushing, deafening rumble of water, air, pressure, force.

I have no idea which way is up, which way is the right way, how far out I am, whether I'm heading towards the shore or open sea. I flail with all my limbs at once, like someone falling through space, hoping to feel something, to orient myself, to find air. The wave still has me in its grip, rushing me forward. Then I feel pebbles grating against my side. I'm rubbed, like sandpaper, along the bottom of the sea. I press my hands, my feet, against it and push off and up, breaking the surface, gasping, coughing, retching.

I lift my head. I'm back, on the beach, in India, in knee-deep water, between sky and sea, in the life I thought I'd left—and barely any time has elapsed at all. I feel as though I've slipped through a fissure, like a person kidnapped by fairies, as if I've been away for years and returned to find that everything has stood still. I crawl forwards, through the surf, spitting out water, pushing wet ropes of hair out of my eyes.

The scene is utterly unchanged. Like Brueghel's Icarus, falling into the waves in the far corner of the painting, my misfortune has not been noticed. Everything is as before: the ladies in the sea, the goats wending their way down the fire-coloured cliffs, the elephant being led up the beach.

I try to stand up but it seems that I can't, not yet, so I kneel in the shallows, letting little harmless waves surge past me, back and forth. I straighten my swimwear, watch the water drawing the blood off my skin and whirling it away, as if it has need of it, as if it has some purpose in mind for it. I look about me, at the mimosa trees showering the ground with their yellow dust, at a cirrus cloud illuminated at its frayed edges, at the borders of the empty towels on the sand, the way their rectangular redness pulses against the ochre earth.

I realise I am going through one of those moments that I have had all my life. It has all the shock and surreality of *déjà vu* but without the hint of foresight. It's as if I am suddenly missing several layers of skin, as if the world is closer and more tangible than ever before. Everything is presenting itself in colours and at a volume so vibrant, so lurid, it's as if a dial has been turned up. The noise of people talking by the path makes me want to cover my ears.

The first time I felt this I was around five. It would have been wintertime because I was wearing pale pink mohair mittens and was buttoned into a woollen coat, the collar of which was a worn, faded velvet. The mittens were threaded through the back of the coat on a length of elastic. (I have, as I write this, the distinct feeling that my grandmother knitted the mittens; this is more than likely.) I was outside the local shop, one hand circling the wooden door handle and I was swinging back and forth, letting my free mittened hand meet the other, then fall away. With each swing, the elastic stretched between the mittens tugged and pulled on my back.

I must have been waiting for my mother, who would

have been inside, buying groceries—this was the mid-1970s, a time when leaving small children on pavements outside shops was perfectly acceptable.

I remember that, as I swung back and forth, something shifted or settled upon me, some extra depth of vision. A sudden recalibration or bifurcation of my perceptions took place. I could see myself both from above and from within. I had a sense of myself as minuscule, inconsequential, a tiny moving automaton in a wide scene, and at the same time I was acutely aware of myself as an organism, a human microcosm. I could feel the interlocking stitches on my mittens pressing into my fingers as they clutched the door handle. I could feel the grain of the wood beneath those endlessly repeating stitches. I heard the crackle of my hair against the inside of my hat, could feel the cold air entering me, tunnelling into my body, and I could see it leaving me in a visible stream. I acquired a simultaneous sense of time as a vast continuum and an awareness that my stretch in it would be short, insignificant. I knew, in that moment, and perhaps for the first time, that I would one day die, that at some point there would be nothing left of me, my mittens, my breathing, my curls, my hat. I felt that conviction for the first time. My death felt like a person standing there next to me.

On the beach in India, as I sit there in the water, something similar is occurring, except it's different, as it is every time. Instead of an intimation of mortality, what is solidifying, taking root inside me, is something else, a welding together of this place with the sensation of a near-miss, an escape from something beyond my control. The feeling of having pulled my head, one more time, out of the noose becomes intermingled with, indivisible from, the mimosa trees, the goats, the wave that turned me over, the toasted-resin smell of cinnamon bark.

I haul myself out of the ocean and stagger up the sand. When Will sees me, sees my bleeding forehead, my grazed side, he leaps to his feet.

"My God," he says. "What happened to you?"

"The sea," I say, inarticulate, flopping down onto the ground. "A wave."

"Are you okay?"

"Yeah." I lift a corner of the towel to dab away the blood. "I'm fine."

CIRCULATORY SYSTEM

1991

Short
saphenous
vein

Outer end of
dorsal venous
arch

'm walking through the littered field of a festival. Strains of music, snippets of conversation, exhaled nimbuses of smoke thread themselves around me. The sun is low in the sky but I can still feel its heat on the round bones of my bare shoulders, the bridge of my nose, the base of my neck. The parched, cracked ground beneath my boots reverberates with a pummelling bass from a distant stage.

I'm looking for my friends. We arranged, months ago, to meet here, in these fields, on this day, at the tail end of summer. It seemed a viable scheme, when we talked about it, perfectly possible to find each other among these hordes, these fast-food vans, these stalls selling tie-dye, embroidered bags and woven socks.

These friends and I have been apart for what feels like a long time, over the long university break. I have been working, as a ticket-ripper, a beer-glass collector, a fetcher, a sorter, a general dogsbody, at an arts venue, where I was required to wear a sweatshirt of leprechaun-hair orange. When the job finished, I tied the sweatshirt in a knot and tossed it to the dog, who has a deep but forbidden love of ripping up fabric, and took off for Spain.

I have slept on trains, swum in river gorges, written postcards to a boyfriend who is far away, working in the States for the summer. And now I am back, in this English field, with my rucksack and dusty boots, looking for my friends. If I don't find them, I won't have anywhere to sleep tonight: they will bring the tent, they promised me. Without it, I'll be under the stars all night.

I walk one way, I walk another. I buy a dry falafel wrap at a food stall and chew it, looking into the faces of everyone who passes by. I climb to the highest point of the field, where people are standing, arms aloft, holding on to the strings of coloured kites, which dip and tug in the air above us. If you erased the kites from the scene, these people would look like visionaries, fanatics, gazing into the sky, arms held up in appeal, in awe.

At the yell of my name, from behind me, I turn and the day is transformed. No longer am I alone, in a field, in late afternoon, with the weight of my rucksack: I am swept up, carried along. Two of my friends seize me by the arms, by the hands. They have been looking all over for me, they say, they were getting worried. But here I am. They divest me of my bag and pull me to a huge tent, illuminated by lights, whole constellations of them, where music stretches at the canvas, vibrates in the guy ropes, where a whole group of people I know are standing, calling to me, waving their hands.

We are hard up against a circular wooden barrier, beyond which two horses in feathered bridles trot tightly around the ring, a bare-chested man standing on their backs. There is the familiar, stiflingly anhydrous scent of sawdust. The man on horseback flips himself, landing with his palms on sleek, mottled haunches. Someone passes around a bag of salted nuts, a tepid water bottle: these, I accept; the frail-papered joint and sweating beer I do not. A girl is shouting in my ear about a dress, a flat, a fish, a trip to London. I can't follow the story, can't connect these nouns in this blizzard of noise. In the narrow corridors of spotlights above our heads, figures on trapezes appear and disappear.

When a man in leather trousers, black fedora and matador's waistcoat takes to the ring, we clap, we cheer. He holds a bristling bouquet of daggers high in the air. When he calls for a volunteer, the boy next to me—I know him well, he goes out with one of my closest friends—claps me on the shoulder and yells, "Over here!" He is drunk, I see, his eyes wild, unfocused. His girlfriend, my friend, frowns, pulls on his sleeve, tells him to stop. I know I could refuse. I could walk away, I could demur, shake my head, step back into the crowd—the moment to do this is now—but when the spotlight scythes through the crowd to find us, I nod. I shuck off my jacket and climb over the barrier into the magnesium glare of the lights.

Why? Impossible to say now. Because I am still only a teenager? Because I am so relieved to be back with my friends, to see that my life with them does exist, that I hadn't dreamt it up? Because sometimes I get weary of being the only sober one in a crowd? Because part of me wants to know what it's like out there, in the heat and the light? Because why not? Why not let a man you've never met, a man you have no reason to trust, throw a fistful of knives at you?

As I walk towards the man, chaperoned by the blinding, quivering disc of light, I realise that he is Spanish, which seems an odd but somehow fitting coincidence, given that I have just this week returned from Spain. Of course he's Spanish, I'm thinking. What else would he be? Also, I'm remembering how much I hate being the focus of attention, how uncomfortable it always makes me, how prickling, how searing it feels to have everyone's eyes upon me. How, as a child, I used to dread the singing of "Happy Birthday," the waxy flare of candles before me, the gaze of so many eyes directed at me; it used to make me want to cover my face, duck under the table, run from the room.

I am guided by a sequinned assistant to a circular board. I am buckled there, by the wrist, by the ankle, and an image of Da Vinci's "Vitruvian Man," four-legged, grave of face, apparently unaware of his nudity, flits through my mind. I think about the day when my faraway boyfriend and I measured our heights and arm spans and discovered that my legs were two centimetres longer than my arms. You go against the theory of human geometry, he'd said, frowning, preparing to measure me for a second time, as if hoping to find this defect ironed out.

I look up, across the ring, to see the man in the fedora flexing his hands, readying his stance. He holds his knives in one hand. In the other, he grips a single blade, by its tip, as if assessing its weight, its heft.

Then the unbelievable happens. The assistant steps towards him with a dark length of cloth. A scarf, I tell myself, a headband. She is going to fasten it about his neck, his forehead, to aid concentration, to make sure he isn't distracted from the task in hand.

She fastens it deftly, quickly, over his eyes.

A blindfold, then.

At this point, I realise I may have made a mistake, taken a grave misstep.

I'm not quite sure, as I stand there, how all this came about. One minute I was alone at a music festival, with nothing more complicated to worry about than where I would sleep that night; now I'm strapped to a board and a sightless man is preparing to throw knives at me. How can this have happened?

The assistant is back beside me. She is holding a hammer in one hand. Her shoulders are broad beneath the flesh-coloured mesh of her costume. Her face is screwed up, serious, her lower lip held in her teeth. Her lipstick is applied, thick as butter, to a line drawn slightly outside her natural lips. It gives her an avid, omnivorous air. I try to look into her eyes, to read my fate there, but she doesn't meet my gaze. Sweat glimmers on her arms, her brow. I want to ask her something, anything. Is this going to be all right? Can you promise me I'll survive? Does he ever make a mistake?

She raps the hammer, once, twice, on the board, down by my ankle, yells an incomprehensible syllable over her shoulder, then ducks out of the way.

The noise is like the approach of an insect, the whirring of tiny wings. A knife appears, seemingly engendered by the air, next to my foot. Its tip is embedded, several centimetres deep, in the board.

I had, I think, up until that point, always believed that circus acts were exactly that—acts. Inherently theatrical, deceiving, duping. Tricked up for the audience, a clever conjuration.

There is no doubt, though, of the authenticity of this

knife. Or this one, appearing at my knee, or this, next to my thigh, the other ankle. There is a formula to it, I realise, a rhythm. The assistant cracks her hammer in the intended place, a judge bringing down her gavel, gives a shout, and the man—an impossible, unthinkable distance away—lets fly. It is an auditory trick, this. The man is listening, intently, behind his blindfold, his head on one side, then throwing at what he divines is the source of the hammering. What a feat, what an ability, to drive a knife through space, through a fuse of sound, to pierce such a specific point.

A knife plucks at my dress, near my waist, producing a scowl on the face of the assistant. She shouts something at the man, in an admonishing tone, out of their usual rhythm. The following knife, up near the chest, gets the same response, and I realise what the assistant is saying: *demasiado cerca*. This phrase I recognise. "Too close." She is ticking him off, like a parent, like a teacher, letting him know he is off course, too close for comfort.

I cannot look to see the man take aim now. My head is filled with the anatomical drawings I had to reproduce, not so long ago, in biology exams. Major veins in blue, major arteries in red, spreading like river deltas through the chest, up the neck, down the limbs, just beneath the casing of skin. The man is *demasiado cerca* to me, to my arteries. He is too close. I look across to where my friends are but I cannot see them outside this girdle of dazzling light; I look down at my feet, which seem very far away, and the sawdust. I try not to recall how it used to be sprinkled on the floors of butchers' shops when I was a child. To soak up, to absorb. How I hated to be taken into those places, always begged to be left outside. The cold, congealed forms that hung from hooks or lay, beached and leaking, inside the chill glass of the cabinet. The fake grass surrounds of the display. The cloying, ferrous air. The fluttering plastic ribbons over the door to the back, concealing whatever might lie beyond.

The assistant is banging her hammer, an unquiet spirit at a seance, near my head, and the noise sets up a ringing in my ear. The tinnitus of the terrified. A knife thuds into the wood by my neck and I think, I may not make it, I may not, and pinned like a lepidopterist's sample, I imagine the scene: the colour, incarnadine, crimson, claret-dark, the pulsing of the gush, the flood, the screams. Another knife enters just above my head, tweaking at my hair.

And then it is over. The assistant is unbuckling me and I am activating my arms, my legs, I am peeling them away from the board and I run, not stopping to acknowledge the applause, away from the light, the assistant, the man, away from the board, where lies a vacancy, a doppelgänger, myself, picked out in blades.

HEAD

1975

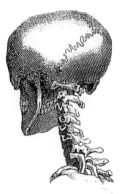

oes a near-death experience I don't remember count?
This one is from my early childhood, a time predating
recall. My mother, of course, tells it to me, as we move
about her kitchen together.

She is making a pot of tea and I am clearing plates
from the table. We both step around the room, around
the dog, around the circular table, around each other, by
instinct. I could navigate this space with my eyes closed,
if called upon to do so. From down the corridor, the voices
of my children, playing with the array of toys my mother
keeps in her cupboards, can be heard, rising and falling,
exclaiming and negotiating.

Tea-making is a sacred, circumscribed ritual in this
house. I would never presume to undertake it, would
never encroach on this most delicate of tasks. There are
several steps that must be followed, one leading myste-
riously from the next: I can never quite remember the
sequence, have always been too impatient to learn, unlike
my sisters, who enact the same ritual in the same way
in their own kitchens.

The correct pot must be selected, as should the most

suitable cosy. Warming must take place, for a prescribed amount of time, and this water must absolutely be discarded, with a quick, derisive flick into the sink. Only then may the tannin-dark pot be filled, first with tea leaves, measured out with a specially appointed pewter spoon, then boiling water. On goes the cosy—knitted or quilted, mostly embroidered—then steeping occurs. On the draining board, cups (bone china, always) and milk at the ready.

My mother places a glass of tap water on the table, in front of the chair that was mine when we were growing up, in deference to my non-tea-drinking habit. She knows I won't partake of what's brewing in the teapot, so she provides me with the only liquid I reliably drink.

I am the sole tea-abstainer in my family. I think they regard this as a baffling perversion. To me, tea tastes like dried lawn-clippings, diluted leaf mould, watered-down compost mixed with a dash of bovine bodily fluid. I have never been able to stomach it.

As she lifts the pot to the table, she asks me what I'm working on at the moment, and, as I swallow my water, I tell her I'm trying to write a life, told only through near-death experiences.

She is silent for a moment, readjusting cosy, milk jug, cup handles. "Is this your life?" she asks.

"Yes," I say, a touch nervously. I have no idea how she will feel about this. "It's not . . . it's just . . . snatches of a life. A string of moments. Some chapters will be long. Others might be really short."

We talk for a moment about what will be included. My childhood illness, nearly being run over, childbirth, dehydration from dysentery. There will be things in the book I have told her about and others I have never mentioned: I don't enlighten her as to these now. She asks if I'll write about having septicaemia, and I say no. I don't remember it. I was too young. And also I don't think I was in danger of dying, was I?

She doesn't answer but turns her head to look out of the window, at the birds who flit and flap around the feeders she hangs from her trees.

"There was that other time," she says, "when you didn't stay in the car. Do you remember?"

"No," I say.

"You were three or so—it was when your sister was a baby. We'd been to the shops and I'd driven the car into the garage. I told you to stay put, to stay in your seat," she gives me a look, almost a nod, "but . . ."

"But I didn't?" I supply.

"No," she says, "you didn't. I had the shopping out and was reaching up to slam the boot shut when I saw you, in that split second. You'd somehow got out and come around to where I was. You were right there, standing beside me, your head in the way of the boot. It nearly got you." She holds up her fingers, narrowly parted. "Nearly, nearly," she repeats. "I hoicked you back just in time. When I think what might have happened if . . ." She doesn't finish her sentence, shaking her head.

There is a short silence in the kitchen. I am thinking that perhaps I should apologise for being the kind of child who never did as she was told, persistently putting herself in the way of danger. I should also thank her for saving me.

There is, of course, no greater fear for a parent than the loss of a child. I know this; my mother knows this. We have both lived it. She and I have both sailed too close, too many times, to those terrifying dark rocks. It's something we share but rarely speak of.

I am still casting about for what to say in response when my children appear, pouring into the room, filling it with talk and shouts and wooden toys and need. Need for drinks, for sliced apples, for scones, for jam and butter.

As I drive home, I think about the story. I have no memory of it at all, which seems strange. You'd think that something so dramatic would leave a mark. Perhaps, I decide, as I drive, my lack of recall is a testament to my mother's handling of the situation. She must have had not only quick reflexes but a way of containing the event, internalising it, so that none of the panic leaked out to me.

I remember the garage, however, a fascinating and slightly frightening place with oil stains, slick and pungent, on the concrete floor, which, if looked at one way, could resolve into rainbows, iridescent and fleeting. It had dark red doors and a window behind which a blue-tit once became trapped, its wings whirring in terror, its black beak driving again and again into the glass, unable to comprehend that it wouldn't yield. My father wrestled with the catch, with the painted-shut sill before it finally gave and the bird flew out, swooped once over the flowerbed, then away over the hedge. I remember it as a cobwebby, dim place, filled with the bladed lawn-mower, the heads of spades, an axe resting on a high nail. A rat was seen in there once, which occasioned a visit from the Rat Catcher, a man with thick, high boots, leather gauntlets, a bottle of poison, an empty hessian bag and a noosed stick. He went into the garage and shut the door; we watched from the sitting room. When he emerged, his bag was no longer empty but weighted down with something curved, slack and soft.

One summer we set up a museum in the garage,

exhibits arranged over workbench and chest freezer. They included the skeleton of our tortoise, disinterred from the ground, some stamps from Malaysia, several trilobites and some pieces of Connemara coral.

Our tabby cat, thrillingly, chose the garage as the place to give birth. We would visit her with her new family, awed and delighted, to worship at the side of the cardboard box, to watch the four squirming bodies as they searched for sustenance in her grey-striped fur.

My mother instructed us not to touch the kittens, not yet, and we nodded gravely. As soon as she had gone back to the kitchen, however, I told my younger sister to keep watch at the garage door. Obviously, I reasoned to her, there was no way I wasn't going to touch these kittens. No way at all. The keen joy of plunging in your hands and lifting up all four kittens in a mewing, writhing mass and burying your face in their aliveness, their softness, their miniature faces, their never-walked on paws: how could I forgo this?

The cat lifted her head and watched me with green eyes that were alert but also absolving. She knew it wasn't possible for me to follow my mother's edict—there was no way I could. She purred when I put the kittens gently back, stretching out an ecstatic paw to touch me on the wrist.

She lived an astonishing twenty-one years, that cat. There are photographs of me holding her as a gawky ten-year-old, with patched knees and teeth too large and numerous for my mouth, and photographs of me as an adult, less gawky, less patched, with her on my lap.

Years later, in the middle of a cold winter, I will be pregnant with my first child and living abroad, snow-bound, in a deep-cut valley. My sister, now a vet, will call to say that the cat, who, a lifetime ago, gave birth to some kittens in a cardboard box, is sick, too sick. She cannot save her this time—the cat won't survive another oper-ation. My sister will be saying sorry and asking me if it's okay to put her down, and I will be saying, of course, whatever you think is right.

She and I will be clutching the ends of our respective phone lines, separated by countries and mountains and seas, reluctant to end the call because we both know what will happen after we do. I will be reminded of the time we were separated by the length of the garage—a place where I had so nearly and unknowingly come to a nasty end—as she stood, a loyal and anxious sentinel, keeping watch, her head turning between me and the house, as I bent over the box and lifted the kittens aloft.

CRANIUM

1998

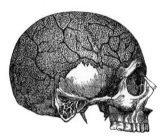

A man and a woman are walking beside a river. The water is so slow-moving as to be almost current-less, motionless. They pause on a bridge, looking down at their reflections in the mirror-flat, leaf-dinted water: he looks at hers, she looks at his. She has been collecting acorns in her pockets, greenish-brown and set inside their cups, and as they have walked, she has sifted them with her fingertips and ascertained that, yes, each acorn will fit only inside its own cup. No other cup will do.

The woman is me. The man is—well, never mind.

They are talking about their situation, their conundrum. They have fallen in love, instantly, surprisingly, dizzyingly, but there are problems. There are obstacles. Other people stand in their way—other hearts, other minds, other situations.

The woman puts out her hand to touch the dry stalk of a reed, as she talks, saying something about how can they, how could they, they could never, could they? The man reaches out to warn her, saying that he was once with a friend who cut his finger so deeply on a reed that he needed three stitches at a cottage hospital.

"A cottage hospital?" the woman repeats. She has never heard of such things. She says she is picturing a hospital with a thatched roof, smoke spiralling out of a chimney, staffed perhaps by squirrels or mice in aprons, picture-book style.

The man raises an eyebrow at her. "They exist. I assure you." He hasn't, she notices, let go of her hand.

They talk about reeds, about stitches, about times they have had them, because they need a break, perhaps, from talking about themselves, about their unresolvable scenario, about options, all of which seem at once unavoidable and yet unconscionable. Still holding her hand, he lifts his shirt to show her a childhood scar on his abdomen; she sees a tanned slice of stomach, the waistband of his underwear riding above his jeans, a line of hair disappearing south. She wants to turn away, she wants to keep looking; she wants to bite him, like a peach. She thinks, how can we? How can we not? This is a bad idea, this is the best idea, the only idea; she is looking for a private, shielded place, she is scanning for a way to make good her escape. The moment seesaws between them.

Suddenly a dog appears, out of nowhere, out of the forest, popping out of the trees like a jack-in-a-box. It has a half-white, half-black face and a waving plume of a tail. It bounds towards them, as if they are the two people it most wants to see in the whole wide world, circling them, leaping and yapping, its tail swishing from side to side, its face split wide in a canine grin.

They exclaim, they bend to stroke it, to run their hands along its warm, furred flanks.

When they walk on, the dog comes too, darting ahead on the path, looping back, diving between them, begging for sticks to be selected, tossed, re-thrown. It thrusts itself past their ankles as they continue to talk, it plunges in and out of the undergrowth, it gazes up at them, panting, adoring, as if rapt by what they are saying, as if signalling its complete agreement.

At one point, the walk takes them along a stretch of road. The dog trots between them, nose down. They hear the grind of a large vehicle behind them so they step to the verge, still talking. A huge orange lorry comes hurtling down the lane, trees flinching away from it, tyres consuming tarmac.

As they wait for it to pass, it occurs to the woman that she has no idea if the dog has any road sense. Some dogs, she knows, do; others don't. The lorry is almost upon them when she bends down to put her hand on the dog's collar, to ensure it doesn't suddenly spring into the road, into the path of the lorry: she is acting entirely by instinct, thinking only of protecting this animal, who has appeared from nowhere, who approaches the world and all it has to offer with such trust, such unalloyed joy. She feels the mechanism, the powered steel of the lorry pass near her—too near. The hair on her head is flicked by the side of the vehicle; she is sensible of the wheel arch skimming the top of her cranium: metal at a considerable velocity just passing over skull. A centimetre, half a centimetre more and it would have hit her square on the head. The horror of this near-decapitation rises, like a tide, from her feet, her legs, rushing over her in a single, distinct sensation. She could have died, right here, right now, holding on to the man with one hand and the dog with the other. A minuscule unit of measurement in the wrong direction and that would have been it. Curtains. Kicked the bucket. Carked it. End of the line. Lights out. Bitten the dust. Gone the way of all flesh. Given up the ghost.

She has never been good at judging the correct distance between herself and other entities, knowing how much space she takes up, how much clearance she needs.

The lorry zooms on. They are caught in its backdraught, the man, the woman, the dog, their bodies overcome by motion, by speed. She straightens up. She releases the dog's collar. She is aware of having dodged something, of having pulled her leg out of the trap, once again, at the last moment.

She says nothing to the man. He does not need to know. There is already so much at stake. He is putting his arm about her shoulders and pressing her to his side, to his chest, to the muscle and bone nearest his heart. She rests her cheek against the woollen nap of his coat and breathes there, picturing the molecules of him, his scent, his skin, his clothes, his hair, drawn down into her lungs, along the pathways and tributaries of her bronchial tubes, her alveoli, dissolving there into her bloodstream and being carried away, sporing and spinning into the most secret junctions of her self.

They walk on, along the road and back into the forest, where the light is patched and green, where the path is winding, diverging, not always clear. The dog comes too.

INTESTINES

1994

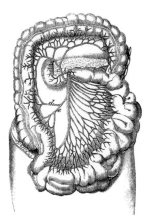

open my eyes to see the French doctor from the restaurant standing over my bed, fists on hips, elbows bent at right angles to her body. I stare at her, astonished, wanting to ask her what on earth she is doing in my room. Has she lost her way? Her mind? Her key? Has she opened the wrong door?

I can't remember how long it is since I chatted to her, over breakfast, how long I've been lying here, ill. Days, certainly—spent prostrate on the unforgiving mattress or crouched in the narrow bathroom—but I have lost track of time by this point, lost track of everything.

She reaches out and touches her hand to my forehead, my arm. I hear her say to Anton, whose face hovers in the background, fearful, dismayed: "She needs to go to hospital."

Since I arrived here, in this small Chinese town, however long ago it was, I have been unwell, unable to eat much, needing to visit the loo with tiresome frequency, feeling enervated, listless, not sleeping. Then I was gripped by sudden pains, in the middle of the night, and started throwing up; I couldn't stop. It woke Anton, who came and held my hair out of the way. What came out of me was streaked with blood, mucoid, meaty in texture.

Something is moving within me, deep in the coiled channels of my stomach, something with claws, with fangs, with evil intent. It is gaining strength, I can feel it, drawing it off me. It is as though I have swallowed a demon, a restive one that turns and fidgets, scraping its scales against my innards. I must fold into myself, breathe, grip my hands into fists until the spasm passes.

And now here is this stranger, this French woman, saying I must go to hospital. It is, I decide, too much. I shut my eyes, aiming to block her out, and Anton, and their plans. It seems to me in this moment that there is nowhere so lovely, so restful, as this painted concrete box of a Chinese hotel room. I don't want to go anywhere. I want to stay right here, on these peach-coloured nylon sheets, with the ceiling fan churning above me, with the curtains shut to keep out the glancing sunlight. Only here can I square up to this demon; only here can I try to gather my resources to face it.

I have reached that dangerous stage in dehydration, in fever, the point where you give up, where you just want to stay where you are, lying curled up on your mattress.

"No," I say, but I can barely raise a whisper. "I'm okay."

"She has to go," the French doctor says, her words

clipped but calm. She isn't talking to me. "It must be now."

They lift me between them—I am light, lighter than I've ever been, I'll discover later, even in my self-whittling teenage years, the flesh melting from me in a matter of days—and I cling to the peach-coloured mattress.

"No," I protest, kicking, delirious, furious, the spiked demon twisting within me. "I don't want to go. I want to stay here. Put me down."

Anton half drags, half carries me through the hotel lobby and out of the glass doors, where a rank of motorised rickshaws is idling at the kerb; the French woman dematerialises, yet another saviour never to be seen again. I don't recall much of the rickshaw ride, other than Anton holding me by the arm as I dry-retch out of the open door. There is, I observe to myself, even through illness and pain, nothing left in my system. Nothing at all—no liquid, no food, no bile, even. I am utterly emptied out. My skin is scalding, desiccated. It hurts to move my eyes inside their parched sockets. But, still, I don't want to go to hospital. I want only to be left alone.

I realise now that what I had hit was the tipping-point. My body, invaded by an amoebic parasite picked up on the Buddhist mountain of Emeishan, had for several days battled for supremacy. I had eaten carefully, I had taken rehydration salts, I had rested. I had done everything you are meant to do when you get travellers' tummy, but this was something different. My fever was raging up in the forties; I had been vomiting and shitting, with increasing frequency, for several days. Every last thing was out of my body. The amoeba was winning. What I thought I wanted was to be left in peace but what this really meant was that I was giving up: I was ready to die, to abandon the fight. It was easier than staying alive.

A Buddhist mountain: I had pictured a steep, mossy incline, hung with mist, a path through bamboo and gongtong forests, a peak disappearing into sky. I had imagined pilgrims in robes, red-painted monasteries with plangent, clanging bells. A scene from the calligraphic brush of a Chinese artist.

The reality isn't far off, if you overlay that image with hordes of pilgrims and tourists, some carried in bamboo sedans by porters, some in astonishing shiny high-heels, inching their way up the stone-cut steps. The path is, in places, so crowded that it becomes necessary to stop and wait for the bottleneck to ease. The steps are uneven and ever-so-slightly too small for an entire foot. I have to watch every one, make sure my toes connect.

Emeishan is one of the four sacred Buddhist mountains

in China, and the highest. It is, according to the battered guidebook that rides in the pocket of my backpack, regarded as a *bodhimanda,* or place of enlightenment. It has no fewer than seventy-six monasteries, one of which was China's first Buddhist temple.

The sacred summit is ten thousand feet above sea level, to be reached by more stone-cut steps. On a bus through the hummocked limestone landscape of Kunming, a man with blond dreadlocks and a tenuously fastened sarong took my fingers in his and told me, with closed eyes, that the climb to the summit of Emeishan is the physical manifestation of a *koan*—a paradox or challenge that leads to enlightenment. I nodded and, after what seemed a decent interval, reclaimed my hand.

Anton is climbing the mountain with me. We have left Hong Kong and are going back to the UK. I am heading for London, where I am hoping to find work on a newspaper or a magazine. I need to start my life: I need to find a path for myself, to find a job that sets me on the right course or, in fact, any course at all. I have to find work that will pay my rent, cover my tube travel, and doesn't bore me to the point of screaming, so that I have the headspace and the energy to come home in the evenings, perhaps, maybe, possibly, to write. But how to pull off such a trick, such a balancing act? I haven't the faintest idea.

So I am heading back to Britain, slowly and circuitously, spinning out the journey for as long as my money will last.

We are travelling overland, through China, through Mongolia, across Siberia, then Eastern Europe, ending up in Prague in a month or two, where there is a twenty-four-hour bus to London. And there the rest of my life will start. Somehow. The Prague bus is as far as my plans go. I have no job, no home in London. I will arrive there in a matter of weeks, to sleep on a friend's floor, armed with cuttings of articles I wrote for Hong Kong news-papers. I am, as I climb the steps of Emeishan, hoping for the best.

When we are hungry, we stop at one of the monasteries along the way. The monks feed us noodles and rice, steamed vegetables, pale squares of tofu. If it's late, they will find us a bed in a dormitory or, if we are lucky, a wood-partitioned room to ourselves. If the humidity becomes too much, we dip our hands, our heads into the ice-cold streams that flow down the mountain. Every now and again, we encounter a phalanx of grey-brown macaque monkeys. A Dutch woman we met at the base of the mountain warned us about these creatures. "They will fly at you," she said, "because they know tourists carry food in their backpacks and they will stop at nothing to get it." She rolled back the sleeve of her sweatshirt to reveal a set of deep scratches, made by sharp, insistent fingernails. "You see?" she said, and we nodded gravely. We did see.

The monkeys sit in the trees, on the tops of walls, lying in wait, watching our approach with intent, shrewd eyes. I remember the technique my sisters and I perfected with a particularly menacing black Labrador that lay across the pavement on our route back from school: I tell Anton that the only way is to get our retaliation in first, to show the monkeys we are bigger and scarier than them, before they have a chance to try anything. He looks doubtful. When we come across a group crouching beside a small pool, eyeing us with a calculating stare, I lunge forward, baring my teeth, stamping my feet, yelling at the top of my voice. The monkeys scatter like marbles, scrambling away from the water's edge, vanishing up trees, around boulders, over walls. The clearing is silent, deserted, the only sound the bubbling of the stream.

"A bit much?" I say.

At the summit, we are woken in the middle of the night by mice that have gnawed through the cotton of my bag and are rustling purposefully about inside a packet of crackers. It's still too early to go outside and watch the sunrise so Anton and I choose this moment to have an argument. We bicker half-heartedly about a range of topics—his refusal to stay in a certain hostel, my loss of temper beside a lake earlier in the week, how I'm always reading instead of talking to him—until I accuse him of being indecisive. We are off: we have the bit between our teeth. He counter-accuses me, in a wholly unprecedented move, of being secretly in love with my friend, the man who gave me the compass, which is currently stowed in the bag the mice have broken into.

There is a moment of shocked, suspended silence in our panelled box of a room as we lie, not quite warm enough, in all of our clothes, under a heap of quilts.

"What," I demand, in an unsteady voice, in the middle of the night, in the oldest Buddhist monastery in China, a sacred place where people come to gain enlightenment, "makes you say that?"

Anton is steely, numeric in his reply. "You write really long letters to him," he tells me. "You're always trying to find phone-boxes to call him. It's odd, you being so close to another man."

"How dare you," I bluster, stumbling from the bed with an outraged flounce, "accuse me of such a thing?"

We watch the sunrise, along with a few thousand other people, who pose for photographs that make it seem as though they are cupping the sun in the palms of their hands. Then we catch the bus down the mountain, and as we travel, side by side, mostly in silence, I begin to feel strange. The petrol fumes from the bus seem to invade my throat, the grind of the steering, the smell from the crate of flapping chickens across the aisle, the creak of the leather seats all conspiring to make me feel headachy, queasy, dizzy. Have I picked something up from the sacred mountain?

Out of the rickshaw and up the hospital steps, Anton supporting me, my arm around his neck. Through the door and we are confronted with a scene from Dickensian London, from a First World War film, from a nightmare. The foyer of the hospital is filled with people: literally, filled. There isn't a chair, a square foot of floor or wall space that isn't taken up by a human form. There must be a hundred, two hundred people crammed into this waiting room. People sit, lined up, along the reception desk; others lie on mats or flattened cardboard boxes on the floor, asleep or just moaning lightly to themselves. Children, cradled in the arms of adults, wail. A man sits, his swollen leg propped on a birdcage, cracking sunflower seeds between his teeth, spitting the shells to the floor.

Beside me, I hear Anton swear softly.

We stand in the doorway for a few minutes, unsure what to do. Should we stay? Should we head back to the hotel? Should we take a seat or rap assertively on the closed window of the reception desk?

A man in a white coat picks his way through the crowd and stops in front of us. He puts a weary hand to my forehead, he pulls up my lips, as if I am a horse, and examines my teeth.

"Stomach?" he says to Anton, in English.

Anton nods.

"You pay?" he asks.

"Yes."

"Dollars?"

Anton digs in my money belt and shows the doctor the wad of my emergency-only American dollars, ordered and collected from a bank in Hong Kong before I left. I hadn't thought I'd ever need them, had almost not bothered to get them, but a woman I worked for had told me I shouldn't go to China without them.

"Okay?" Anton asks.

The doctor nods, takes me by the arm, leads me through the maze of people.

I am hooked up to a drip, using a needle from a medical kit I bought in Kowloon: there is a minor tussle about this, between me and the nurses. I am given antibiotics to rid me of the parasite, enormous mustard-coloured tablets I have to wash down with huge gulps of water. They flush out the amoeba, along with most of my gut lining. In a few months, when I am living in London, I will be sent to the Hospital for Tropical Diseases because I am still pale, anaemic, still losing weight. The doctor there will ask me what medication I was given and, when I tell her, she'll blanch.

"What?" I will say. "What's wrong?"

"Those are only used here for . . ." She stops herself.

"For what?" I ask.

"Well . . ." she frowns at her screen ". . . horses."

I stare at her. Then I laugh.

The doctor shrugs. "They worked, I guess. I mean, you're still here."

In several more years, I will be travelling in South America with Will. In a hotel room in La Paz, I will be woken by nausea, by fever, by an all-too-familiar scraping, clenching, serpentine pain. I eat a banana and it passes through my digestive system in thirty-two minutes: I time it on my watch. I will shake Will awake.

"I think I've got another amoeba," I'll say to him, through set teeth.

"Huh?"

"An amoeba. As in amoebic dysentery."

He will go out in the early morning into the streets of La Paz to find a pharmacy, armed with a piece of paper, inscribed with the name of an equine antibiotic.

BLOODSTREAM

1997

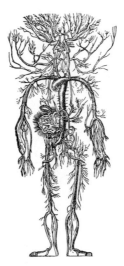

Occasionally, but not that often, I think about the person I was in my mid-twenties. I consider her. I try to recall how it felt to be that age. What were the frameworks of her days, the patterns of her thoughts? I am as far from her now as she was from her childhood. She is the median line between me and my birth.

Sometimes it's hard to capture her essence, impossible to remember what it was like to keep forging ahead in the face of such flux and instability. Other times, however, I might be walking down a street with my children, holding one by the hand while trying to catch up with another and simultaneously listening to what the third is saying about the Scottish referendum (my children have divergent and incompatible walking styles—one likes to lag behind, another to sprint ahead, and the other to walk right next to me, so close that I'm often tripped by our tangling feet). We will be moving along in our assorted fashions, when I will be hooked by something—the specific timbre of a decelerating underground train, a particular guitar riff coming out of the window of a basement café, the feeling of cold fingertips curled inside a pocket—and I will sense her as if she is on the pavement with us.

There she goes, walking by, in her weather-insufficient tights, short skirt and bright blue trainers. She has cut off her hair—it doesn't entirely suit her—and bleached the asymmetric fringe. She has a pager in her belt, a book in her bag and a lidless pen leaking ink into the lining. She walks fast; she is probably late. She needs a multivitamin, a square meal, a place to live. She has moved no fewer than nine times since she arrived in London. She can fit her possessions into a single backpack. She gets sore throats, swollen tonsils. She stays out late, doesn't sleep much, fails to purchase even the most basic of groceries. She runs out of money before payday every month.

She has recently left the man she'd been living with, shouldering her bag and walking down the stairs. The circumstances were dismayingly pedestrian, soap-operatic in their mundanity: she had knelt beside the bed to search for a shoe and seen instead the loop and catches of a bra. She knew before she touched it. A flesh-coloured bra, not her size, not a style she ever wore, bought from a shop to which she had a particular aversion. A surprisingly practical bra, under the circumstances—no wiring, no embellishment—and ingrained with the sanitised scent of fabric softener. The kind of bra that a sporty, organised, no-nonsense girl might wear under a smart blouse. A girl who does her laundry on a regular basis, buys clothes to last and takes herself on healthy outdoor excursions. A girl who is, in short, her diametric opposite, in every way.

She confronted him, in a lowered voice, so as not to alert their flatmates to the situation. At first her boyfriend tacked wildly. He'd never seen the bra before, it was nothing to do with him. He had no idea where it had come from. It was probably hers. Could she have forgotten she'd bought it? It belonged to a visitor. It arrived here by mistake. It must be his sister's.

Pausing in the act of cramming sweaters and dresses and books into her bag, she laughed. Bullshit, she said loudly, momentarily forgetting the other people in the rooms around them. That, she pointed at the bra, flung wide on the boyfriend's desk, wouldn't fit your sister in a million years.

He stopped disowning the bra. He stood up. He got defensive, angry. He said, yes, all right, there has been a woman. There have, in fact, been several. He accused her of always working or reading or sitting at her desk writing (or, as he put it, "typing"). She never had any time for him. If she wasn't out, she was distracted by something else. He was losing his sense of self, his sense of worth, and needed to find himself again. He ended this speech with the words: "I did it for us."

This closing sentence has provided her and her friend Eric with much comedic mileage during the more boring moments of their jobs (of which there are many). They like to tack the phrase on to acts of an entirely self-serving nature, the more selfish the better. Extra points are awarded for slipping it into conversation in front of a more senior colleague, which isn't hard to do because pretty much everyone is senior to them.

"I ate a sandwich," Eric will murmur into his phone from across the office, "and I did it for us."

"I bought some new shoes in my lunch-hour," she will message him, "for us, of course."

"I went to the gym last night," he will say in a loud voice, "and I want you to know that I did it for us."

It has been two years since she got off the twenty-four-hour bus from Prague in a damp bus station in London. It has taken her this long to find a job that doesn't seem like a cul-de-sac. She is working as an editorial assistant on a newspaper. She answers phones, she opens post, she calls critics to remind them that their copy is due, she tracks down the IT man if computers misbehave, she fetches page proofs, she checks captions, she visits the picture desk to find photographs, she tidies—cupboards,

shelves, in-trays, chairs, desks, drawers. She does whatever people ask of her and, in return, she badgers them
gently, politely, to let her write something for the paper.
She counsels editors, assistant editors, critics, sub-editors
on the phone, in the smoking room, in the alcove by the
photocopier that everything is going to be all right. It is
a job with long hours, indistinct boundaries, diva-ish
personalities, twists and turns of panic, steep learning
curves, feverish in-house gossip, urgent deadlines, days
with no lunch and then days when she is taken out of
the office for hours at a time by an older colleague, who
will ply her with expensive food, then quiz her about
something that's happening in her section. Her days are
filled with changes of management, made over everyone's
heads, dry sandwiches, redundancy paranoia, coffee
machines, security passes, rides in lifts, slews of book
proofs, late-night tube rides home at the end of press day,
peculiar freebies (a reflective bag, paperweights with the
heads of authors inside, wellington boots that don't quite
fit, chocolate toolkits and once, out of the blue, an aston-
ishingly expensive German fountain pen—which I still
have).

So, her ex is right, in a way. She is out at work a great
deal. She is distracted. When she is at home, which isn't
often, she is usually writing ("typing"). She has started

something that she is telling herself is a short story. Just a short story. It is, the last time she checked, more than twenty thousand words and getting longer all the time. When she meets her friend Will for a coffee—they are friends at this point, good friends, very good friends, friends who call each other every day, who see each other once or twice a week, friends who perhaps take a shade too much interest in the ups and downs of each other's love lives—and he asks her what she's been writing, she tells him about her short story, her long short story. He looks at her, in his penetrating way, narrowing his eyes, and says: you're writing a novel.

No, she says, shaking her head, of course not, I could never do that, absolutely not, whatever gave you that idea?

Late at night, when her soon-to-be ex-boyfriend calls for her to come to bed, for God's sake, she murmurs absently, in a minute. The house is so quiet, the flatmates all asleep, the work of the story so absorbing, so satisfying in a way that nothing else ever has been, the words scrolling out from under the flashing cursor, the paragraphs opening out from each other, like Matryoshka dolls. Then, suddenly, it's three a.m. and she's blindsided by exhaustion and exhilaration, and she crawls into bed, thinking about her story, unable to find the path to sleep, listening to the sounds of the city waking up.

. . .

She has waited the requisite time: she knows it takes months for the virus to appear in your blood. (Does it hide somewhere, she wonders, like a pantomime villain, behind a door, up a chimney, in the leaves of a tree?) As with anyone who grew up in the 1980s, she knows the rules, the risks, the causes. She still remembers the grim governmental warnings on TV, with falling tombstones and rock-flaying chisels.

So, she is taking herself off to a clinic for the blood test. Not a prospect to relish, this, but something to be got through. She wants to be sure that her ex-boyfriend hasn't passed anything on to her, hasn't deposited anything sinister in her bloodstream.

She has persuaded Eric to come with her, to get tested alongside her. Eric walks the distance from the tube station to the clinic door, talking, gesturing, tugging at the ends of her scarf.

At the clinic, there is an administrative fluster. The receptionist cannot countenance that Eric has arrived without an appointment. "The thing is," he said, snatching off his sunglasses, "my need is greater than hers."

She sees the receptionist about to argue, to insist, to stick to her guidelines and to deny him a test, but then she sees her look at Eric, properly and for the first time.

There is a slight pause.

The receptionist nods, finally, to the pile of forms and they walk away together, towards the waiting area.

"'Write down a list of the people you have slept with in the past five years'," Eric reads aloud from the form—a little too aloud. "Do you think you're allowed to ask for extra paper? Like in an exam?"

"Ssh," she says, and he is saying an affronted "What?" and she is trying not to laugh because it seems a sacrilegious thing to do here, in a sexual-health clinic, where other people are sitting with their heads bowed, avoiding each other's eyes, working their way through these labyrinthine forms.

Eric sighs, fidgets, says they need to line up some sort of treat for afterwards. "What if you don't know their names?" he is asking, tapping his pen on the clipboard. "Do you just write Man One, Man Two? Or, if I'm being brutally honest, Man Ninety-nine, Man One Hundred?"

At that moment, someone calls her name and she gets up, lifting her clipboard, and walks towards a woman in a green overall. Eric is behind her, hissing that he isn't going to let her forget she made him do this, that she put him through it, even though she knows how much he hates needles. She moves in her blue trainers over the carpet, and as she does so, she considers the gravity of the possible outcome. Could it be that her ex has passed on something destructive, something stealthy and corroding? That his body scooped up something from the wearer of the flesh-coloured bra—or one of the others—and deposited it in hers? She hasn't allowed herself to dwell on who these women were, whether she knows them, whether they looked at her clothes draped on the chair, her books stacked up beside the bed, her make-up and toothbrush in the bathroom, the photos on the walls of her sisters, her nieces, her coat hanging by the door, whether they thought, I wonder who she is. She tries not to imagine them, what they looked like, how he touched them, what they might have said together, how he could not have said anything the first time it happened, how he could turn from them to her, without giving himself away. Infidelity is as old as humanity: there is nothing about it you can think or say that hasn't been thought or said before. You go back and back over the days, the conversations, the walks you took, wondering why on earth you hadn't seen it, how you could have missed it, how you could not have known. The pain of it is interior, humiliating, infinitely wearying.

She knows this; Eric knows this. It's why they joke about it all day long, with a gleeful irreverence that probably annoys everyone else in earshot. Sometimes being flippant is the only way forward, the only way to get through.

Perhaps this attitude, however, has been preventing her from entertaining the possibility that these tests might be positive. She realises this as she walks towards the nurse. She made this appointment mostly for show, so she could tell Eric as she dialled the number, so he could listen as she made the appointment, so she could say to him, as she headed out from work, why don't you come too? You could keep me company. We could take the blood test together.

She is on a tightrope as she makes her way to the consulting room, Eric behind her, the nurse in front. What, she is asking herself, will she do if something comes up on this test? If her show-appointment turns out to be needed after all? She tries out the scenario of going round to see her ex. She thinks about taking the tube and walking the very familiar route past the cricket ground, across the bus terminus, ascending the stairs to the door whose threshold she swore she'd never cross again and saying—what, exactly? I need to talk to you? I've got some news for you? What would anyone say in these situations? How do you broach such a subject?

But mostly, as she rolls up her sleeve, as she makes a fist, as she turns her head away—because she never likes to see the needle slide in, the flesh yield beneath its point—she's not thinking about her ex or the other women or the flat they used to share. She's not thinking about the plants she had to abandon there, plants she's sure he never waters, the walls she painted, the curtains she installed, standing precariously on a stepladder to do so. She's thinking about Eric, about his ochre-tinged skin, the cornflake-sized scab on his face that won't heal, the opal-pale moons of his fingernails as he types across the office from her. She is seized with an irrational urge to say to the nurse, make it all right. Please. For him. Make it okay.

CAUSE UNKNOWN

2003

There is no getting around it. The baby is in earnest, his cries coming thicker and faster. He is writhing around within the confines of his car-seat, his face screwed up and scarlet with hunger, with need.

"Can you pull over?" I murmur.

We are on a long, deserted stretch of French road. On one side is a thicket of maize, unmoving in the still, heated air, on the other a wide stretch of sea, some dunes, covered with scrubby, dense undergrowth.

Will steers the car to the verge, pulls up the handbrake. I squeeze through the seats to retrieve the baby from the back seat, and Will says, "I'll just walk down to the sea for a bit."

I'm negotiating the fastenings of an unfamiliar baby seat, easing tiny, angry limbs out of black straps, cradling the vulnerable skull of my son, making sure I don't drop him as I lever myself back into the passenger seat, so I'm not really thinking about what Will has just said, when I say: "Fine."

The baby is furious, ravenous, fists and legs pumping with outrage. I am grappling—juggling, really—with my shirt buttons, the clips of my feeding bra, a muslin square, a breast pad. It is hot and the baby and I are sweaty, slick. Quite a skill, this: the tessellation of two body parts, the docking of jaw with breast. I still haven't got the hang of it, not yet. I have watched others do it, in cafés, on buses, in the fitting rooms of shops. The smooth, upwards motion of it, their lack of fuss, their ease, the way their babies don't seem to move or twist, happy to remain there, peacefully feeding, and I stare at them, covert, envious, wondering how they do it, how they pull it off, and will I ever be as good as that? I never seem to get it quite right, always seem to be ham-fisted, flustered, my son slippery as an eel in my novice grasp.

We give it a try and the baby is so desperate he goes for it with a sudden, snapping pounce. My hands curl with pain. There is no one to hear me cry out. I press my fingers to my forehead, hum to myself, wait for the agony to pass.

We are in France for two weeks. I'm not sure what impulse drove me to book a holiday when my baby would be only nine weeks old but that was back in the before, when I was still pregnant, when I had imagined wafting about in the summer heat, a baby on my hip, seeing friends, visiting galleries, reading, perhaps working, going about my life undisturbed.

The truth is that my life is nothing like this. The truth is that I am not doing so well. I am having trouble keeping my head above water. I did not have the natural birth we all dream of, in a quiet, dark room at home, labouring away, aided only by spritzes of essential oils and soft-voiced doulas. I had a series of interventions in an understaffed, over-lit hospital ward, a long and frightening labour that went on for days and nights, then an emergency C-section that went awry: the baby became stuck, his heart rate dropped, I lost a lot of blood. I was patched up and sent home. The truth is that, just over two months ago, this baby and I nearly died. The resulting scar across my abdomen looks, according to my sister, "like a shark bite."

The truth is that I cannot sleep, even when the baby isn't feeding. When I do manage to sleep—on the sofa, sitting up in a chair—I am beset by short, frantic dreams where someone is committing violence upon me, upon my baby, or dreams where someone has wrenched him from my arms, or where I look over at the Moses basket or the pram and it's empty. I try to walk upstairs and find that I can't, my head swimming and fizzing on the sixth or seventh step. I can't wander to the park. I can't drag myself along the road to the shop. My son and I regard each other in the shaded two ground-floor rooms of our flat while a heatwave surges around the outside walls. My friends come round and it's as if I can't hear them, as if they're behind glass or under a body of water; they seem so far away, sitting across the room. How was the birth? people ask, a kind and eager look on their faces, and I have no idea what to say.

The feeding goes on all day, all night; the baby seems hungry, but halfway through he will rear back, his knees drawn up, his face contorted with pain, with dismay, and then he will howl, he will scream, he will yell for hours and hours, until it's time to feed him again.

Something is wrong, I know. Maybe it's me. Maybe my milk is no good, too much or not enough. Maybe I'm not doing this right. Maybe I'm just rubbish at it. But I'm so wary of doctors, of forms, of hospitals, so rehearsed in the way they can suck you in, chew you up and not spit you out for a long time, that when I see the health visitor, I pull my face into a smile and say, everything's fine. Yes, all good. No, I don't cry more than usual. Yes, he's wonderful, yes, he sleeps, yes, I'm absolutely fine.

In several months' time, I will be at a doctor's surgery in the town where I grew up, waiting for my mother to come out of an appointment, and I will be trying to feed my son. He will be doing his stopping and starting, his rearing, his screaming, his writhing, his knee-jerks; I will be doing my back-patting, my moving around, my latching him on in an upright position and I will walk back and forth while I do this, because he can only feed if he's in motion. I will be clutching his now considerable six-month-old form as I pace up and down, turning and turning when I meet a wall, like a long-distance swimmer. A woman will walk by, regarding us with sidelong interest. I will ignore her, trying to soothe my child, lugging him from one wall to another, coaxing him back on the breast. She will walk by us again, giving me a smile.

"Hello," she will say. "I'm a breast-feeding counsellor. Does your baby always feed like this?"

I will answer by bursting into tears.

Within seconds, I am in her office and she is holding my son. I'm trying to explain that I'm not a patient at this practice, that I live in London, that I'm only here with my mother, but the woman is shrugging, smiling, saying it doesn't matter. She asks me about my son, and I tell her that he starts well but then jerks back. He seems to get a sudden pain halfway through. I tell her I have to feed him at home, always, because we can't do it in public, and I have to unplug the phone and disable the doorbell because any noise at all can disturb him and cause hours of screaming. I tell her all of this, which for me seems normal, but the act of speaking it makes me realise that it's not normal at all.

"So you stay at home with him?"

"Yes."

"Just for feeds or between feeds as well?"

I think about this. "Well, between feeds he's usually . . ."

"Crying?"

I nod.

"So you feed him, or try to feed him, then he cries and after that?"

"I try to feed him again."

She bounces him up and down on her knee, making him smile, making him grab for her necklaces. "Does he bring the milk back up?"

I shake my head.

"I think," she says to him, and he listens to her, rapt, "you've got gastro-oesophageal reflux. They sometimes call it silent reflux but I don't know why because it's anything but. The bad news is that there's nothing you can do about it, but the good news is that it goes away by itself at around six months and I would say," she lifts him high in the air, "you're almost there." She waggles her head from side to side. "So you're going to be fine. More than fine. The question now," she still addresses him, "is what we're going to do about Mummy. Because Mummy's been doing a wonderful job looking after you, but now she needs a bit of help too, doesn't she?"

But this is all to come. Right now, my son is nine weeks old and I'm finding my way, blundering forward with this new job, this new life. Right now, I'm in France, for reasons that are no longer clear to me, trying to breastfeed in a hot car by the side of the road. Right now, Will has disappeared over the dunes to look at the sea, and two men are rustling their way out of the maize field on the other side of the road.

I see them from a long way off. My son has finally settled to the feed and I'm holding myself as still as possible so as not to disturb him, so as not to set off one of his episodes of pain and screaming.

They are carrying bedding rolls on their backs. Their clothes are torn, sun-bleached, their skins tanned brown. One has peroxide-white hair, the other a straggly pony-tail. They are looking at the car, conferring, deciding. They cross the road without looking because it is the kind of road where you can do that: empty, quiet, deserted.

I watch their approach along the dusty asphalt. They are straight ahead of me now, obscuring the vanishing point. I glance over towards the beach. Where is Will? Can he see them coming? Would he hear me if I called?

There is no sign of him. The men are getting closer. They are walking faster; their eyes bore into me, into the car. One is wearing flip-flops; the other walks in bare soles over the hot road.

I cast my eyes towards the ignition. Could I simply drive away? Lay my baby on the seat and hit the accelerator, come back for Will later? The ignition is empty: Will has taken the car keys with him. I reach out my hand to depress the door lock but there isn't one. I scan the dashboard of the unfamiliar rental car. There must be a button that locks all the doors but I can't see it. There are air-conditioning controls, dials to make the car hotter or cooler, switches to bring the windows up or down. There are endless controls for the sound system, settings for CD, for cassette, for more volume, for less.

I am scrabbling around now, my son fallen off the breast, and he is wailing, a high-pitched note of dismay, aghast at the interruption, and the men have seen my panic, seen my problem, and now they are running and I have no idea what they want—money, car, baby, woman—but I don't want to find out, I don't need to know the answer to that question because maybe they don't even know themselves. Maybe they're just ready to react and exploit whatever they'll find here. Still I fumble over the car controls, still my son yells, still the men come, bearing down on us.

Just as they reach the outermost point of the car—so

close they could put out their hands and touch the curve of the bonnet—my fingers find, down near the door handle on the driver's side, a button with the symbol of a padlock. There is a deep, chiming clunk from all five doors of the car. Locked.

The men reach the car. They yank at the doors, front and back, they flatten their palms against the window, they peer in at me, sitting there, one breast exposed, a flailing baby in my arms. The car rocks from side to side but I continue to sit, contained, safe, moated inside metal and glass. I look into their eyes—wild, they are, and blue as the cold, cold sea—I look at the striating lines of their palms, pressed white to the windows. I am panting, they are panting.

One slaps the roof in frustration, in fury. It produces a low note, like that of a bassoon. Then they leave, walk away, rejoining each other at the far end of the car, drifting over the road, melting back into the stalks of maize.

LUNGS

2010

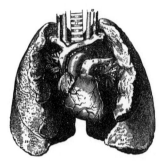

As soon as the water gets too deep for my son, I take him on my back and we half wade, half swim in tandem, him gripping my shoulders with his small hands.

We are wading out to a platform some distance from the shore; another guest at the hotel told us it was "easily walkable." My son and I have been sitting on this African beach, in the shade of a palm tree, all morning, and now the baby is asleep on a towel, watched over by my husband, so my son and I have gone on this aquatic adventure.

I am here to write a travel piece about sustainable tourism in East Africa. We have flown into Tanzania, seeing the white summit of Kilimanjaro piercing up through the thick fleece of clouds. We have taken a small, rattling plane to land on a strip of road between banana trees on Zanzibar. We have walked through spice forests in leech-proof socks, slept in rush-woven huts, climbed the zigzagging steps of a lighthouse on an uninhabited island, searched the vegetation for a rare and reclusive species of deer.

This press trip ends with two incongruous days at a resort hotel, a place more luxurious, more lavish than

I AM, I AM, I AM

anything I have ever seen before. Not a great deal of sustainability to be found here. Men in white jackets rise at dawn to rake the seaweed off the sand. Dried leaves are removed from trees with something that looks like a vacuum cleaner. If you sit on a chair, someone materialises at your side with a tray of cool drinks. If your gaze happens to fall on the azure water of the pool, you will be offered a towel. Things happen around you, unseen, as if benign and house-proud poltergeists are at work: fresh flowers appear at your bed, your hand towels assume the shape of a swan, your clothes are rehung, refolded, rearranged. My son cannot believe it and neither can I. I spend a great deal of my time thanking people for tasks I wouldn't expect anyone to perform for themselves, let alone on my behalf.

It is a relief to be in the sea. No one is in danger of rushing towards me with an ice-bucket, a finger-bowl, a complimentary tray of hand-made chocolates. No one is trying to clean the sea. The water is a clear turquoise, the sand white; shoals of tiny fish arrow and tack around my legs, first one way then the other. The platform bobs before us, tantalising, almost airborne.

I didn't fly in an aeroplane until I was in my last year at school, when I went on a Latin class trip to Italy. Arriving in Rome, age seventeen, was like receiving a blood transfusion. On the bus from the airport, I was assailed, astonished, by the colours of the city—the pale ochre stones of the buildings, the relentless blue of the sky, the green scooters, the tarnished gold of the coins, the black hair of the men who gestured at us, as we stared out of the bus window, smacking their lips. Mesmerising to me were the plates of spaghetti and basil, the baskets of salt-less bread, the strange, lumpy pillows, the shutters over the windows, the noise of car horns, the clitter-clatter of street crossings, and the plush-vowelled language, with its arpeggio dips and peaks. The Spanish Steps, the fountain in the shape of a boat, the pink house where the poet died, the shape of the Colosseum, like an orthodontist's cast of a mouth. I had never seen anything like it. I loved it all to the point of pain. I was dumbstruck, on the constant verge of tears, devastated by the idea that I would have to go home at the end of the week, and this place, these piazzas, these lives, would carry on without me. I wanted to see everything, go everywhere, never to return home.

We were taken around Rome and then to Pompeii, where I put my hand to the groove in a two-thousand-year-old drinking fountain, worn smooth by long-dead people leaning into the jet of water, seeking to slake their thirst. We were let loose among the winding paths of Capri; we climbed to the smouldering summit of

Vesuvius, in mostly unsuitable footwear, the gummed edges of my shoes hoarding grains of volcanic ash. I would find them later, at home, scattered across the carpet of my bedroom. I would pick them up, carefully, obsessively, saving them in a glass jar: my own piece of Italy.

That school trip not only fed but gave a focus to the restlessness I'd felt all my life. At last I had found a way to satisfy it, to meet it; at last I understood it. It had baffled and confounded me for years, the dissatisfaction, the constraint of the everyday, the tedium and scratchiness of routine, the irritating prickle of sameness.

When *Alice's Adventures in Wonderland* was read to me and Alice sighs, "Oh, how I long to run away from normal days! I want to run wild with my imagination," I remember rising up from my pillow and thinking, yes, yes, that's it exactly. The school trip showed me that it was possible to ease this longing, to sate it. All I had to do was travel.

After he had sailed around the Mediterranean in 1869, Mark Twain said that travel was "fatal to prejudice, bigotry, and narrow-mindedness." Neuroscientists have been trying for years to pin down what it is about travel that alters us, how it effects mental change.

Neural pathways become ingrained, automatic, if they operate only by habit. They are highly attuned to alterations, to novelty. New sights, sounds, languages, tastes, smells stimulate different synapses in the brain, different message routes, different webs of connection, increasing our neuroplasticity. Our brains have evolved to notice differences in our environment: it's how we're alerted to predators, to potential danger. To be sensitive to change, then, is to ensure survival.

Professor Adam Galinsky, an American social psychologist who has studied the connection between creativity and international travel, says that "Foreign experiences increase both cognitive flexibility and depth and integrativeness of thought, the ability to make deep connections between disparate forms."*

I sensed this, at an instinctive level, at age seventeen. That unassailable flood of novelty, the stimulus of uncharted territory, the overload of the unfamiliar, with all synapses firing, connecting, signalling, burning new pathways. I have never forgotten that bus ride from the airport into the centre of Rome, my first sighting of the city. And I have never lost the thrill of travel. I still crave the mental and physical jolt of being somewhere new, of descending aeroplane steps into a different climate, different faces, different languages.

* Brent Crane, "For a more creative brain, travel," *The Atlantic*, 31 March 2015.

It's the only thing, besides writing, that can meet and relieve my ever-simmering, ever-present restlessness. If I have been too long at home, stuck in the routine of school-runs, packed lunches, swimming lessons, laundry, tidying, I begin to pace the house in the evenings. I might start to cook something complicated very late at night. I might rearrange my collections of Scandinavian glass. I will scan the bookshelves, sighing, searching for something I haven't yet read. I will start sorting through my clothes, deciding on impulse to take armfuls to the charity shop. I am desperate for change, endlessly seeking novelty, wherever I can find it. My husband might return from an evening out to discover that I have moved all the furniture in the living room. I am not, at times like this, easy to live with. He will raise his eyebrows as I single-handedly shove the sofa towards the opposite wall, just to see how it might look. "Maybe," he will say, as he unlaces his shoes, "we should book a holiday."

Ever since that school trip, I have travelled as much as I can, whenever time and money allow. I was determined that having babies would not change that. I wanted to bring up my children to be travellers, to be curious about the world, to experience other cultures, other places, other sights. I would, I was sure, strap them on to me and off we'd go.

My son was a tiny baby when he first flew in an aeroplane; he was one and a half when I took him to live in Italy, where everyone assumed he was a girl because of his red coat and yellow curls. This trip, age seven, is his first outside Europe.

We are still making our way to the platform, which doesn't seem to be getting much closer, and we are talking about the line of breaking waves that we can see in the distance. I am telling my son that there is a coral reef circling the island, that the seabed is quite shallow until you get out there, when I feel the sandy bottom of the sea fall out beneath my feet.

I pedal my legs, treading water, keeping us afloat. My son is still talking in my ear, still holding on to my shoulders, unaware that we are now no longer walking.

I eye our destination, the platform. I estimate that I can probably make it. The man we met said it was walkable, after all, didn't he? Maybe I've just hit a deep patch, a hollow, and I'll find higher ground again.

So I continue, swimming now, with my son on my back. He has been having lessons back at home, lining up on the side of a London pool with the other children, bathing caps on. I am always able to pick him out by the shape of his neck, the arch of his brow, the stoically anxious expression on his face as he rises out of the chlorinated water. He can do half a width, he can float on his back, he can retrieve plastic sharks from the pool floor. What he can't do yet is swim, here, in open water like this.

I swim and swim, my arms working, my legs kicking behind me. I focus my gaze on the platform, which is rising and falling before me, its silver steps leading up to safety. Every now and again, I stretch down my leg to see if I can touch the bottom. I can't.

I keep swimming. The muscles in my arms and legs are burning, tiring. My son clings to my shoulders, oblivious, chatting, exclaiming. I have to keep reminding him to kick his legs, like his swimming teacher taught him, to help me out.

He can't swim, is what is going round and round in my head. He can't swim. He can't swim and I've brought him out here because of what someone told me. He can't swim, and I've brought him out into deep sea on the advice of an idiot.

Actually, it's me who is the idiot. I grew up near the coast, with a lifelong sea-swimmer for a father, who would call out to us, when we were paddling or practising front crawl in the shallows of the Irish Sea, the same sentence: "Stay in your depth!" Always those words would ring in my ears, *stay in your depth*, but being the child I was, I used to take great pleasure in stepping just that little bit too far, feeling the stones and sand of Donegal beaches fall away from my toes, until I'd hear his voice calling me back.

I should know better. Have I never heard of tides, of water depth changing, of the sea's unpredictability, of sand banks that dip suddenly and steeply away? Have I allowed myself to be so lulled, so infantilised by the ever-present, always anticipated service of this luxury resort that I have surrendered my free will, my judgement? What kind of a mother am I, putting myself and my child in danger like this? I am chiding myself, cursing myself, as I swim, flailing now, all notion of strokes gone, just trying to stay afloat. I go under, the weight of my child pressing me down, but I struggle back and I hear my son, still talking.

It seems very important not to let on, not to communicate to him that we are in trouble, that we might not make it. I don't need to turn my head to know that my husband is too far away to help, and how could he leave the sleeping baby, anyway? If he dived in to rescue us, she might wake up, she might cry, she might—God forbid—crawl towards the water.

All in all, it is an impossible situation and I am the worst kind of idiot. What I would give now to be back on the beach, to be back at home, in London, with both my children safe and sound, never to have seen this place, this beach, this distant platform, never to have met that guest who told us we could walk it, never to have loitered with him by the breakfast buffet.

I go under again, my arms now so weak that they have no traction on the water. I have no muscle strength, no stamina; I have damaged quadriceps, inhibited reflexes, enervated bi- and triceps. What was I thinking? We're going under, it's happening, my eyes smart with salt, my head is subsumed by choking, foamy sea. Is my son above the waterline or is he down here with me? I can't tell. What I see, however, through the greenish, sun-shot depths of the saline water, is the base of a ladder. Two silver steps, which appear, then disappear. Appear then disappear.

I give a kick with my legs, two, I stretch out my hand. I miss. I kick again, stretch, and this time I reach it. I grasp the bottom rung, I pull myself towards it. I haul us up out of the water.

The light, the noise of the waves, the sound of my son, still, incredibly, talking, rush in on me. He climbs off me and up the ladder onto the platform, where he runs from one side to the other, exclaiming. I hook my arms around the ladder, and breathe and breathe and breathe.

CEREBELLUM

1980

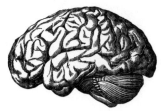

Just before the end of the summer holidays, I woke up early and the world looked different. The colours of the rug, the curtains, the lampshade were more vibrant: they were pulsing, like a heart, like a sea anemone. The bedroom appeared to be suddenly at an angle, the floor tilting, the windows cantilevering into the outside. The ceiling was like a film of floating liquid above me, a distant and blurred meniscus, and I was far below, in some mysterious depth. Nothing was static. Everything shimmered and shifted. I had the sense that my sister, in the lower bunk, was miles away.

For a while, I lay there, arms by my sides, and took it in. The light, the colour, the motion. O brave new world.

After watching my bedroom dissolving and re-forming, I went to get up but when I raised myself off the pillow a sensation burst open inside my head. It was a pain so severe, so pure, that it was as if someone was sounding a high soprano chord somewhere behind my eyes. It was a pain that stretched my head to bursting point, as if my skull was a balloon overfilled with water. It was a pain that had colours—white, yellow, streaks and jags of red—

and a personality. It was like being in the company of a needy, irascible person, who insisted on embracing me too tightly, yakking in my ear, who never left me alone for a moment, who took over my life, who spoke for me and never let me go.

I have never felt pain like it, before or since. It was edgeless, it was perfect, the way the shell of an egg is perfect. And it was invasive, colonising: it sought, I knew, to take me over, to replace me with itself, like a bad spirit, like a fiend.

A day or so later, the pain intensified, gained strength and focus, and it seemed to me that my hands were acquiring minds of their own. They began to waver and swing, like the limbs of the tow-headed, dirndl-wearing puppet that hung from our bedroom ceiling. I reached across the sink for my toothbrush and somehow my hand connected instead with the wall, with the air, with the wall again. I tried to pick up a pencil but my fingers refused to grip. Messages from my brain, from the part of myself I then thought of as my soul, didn't seem to be reaching the relevant limb. Transmission lost.

"Look," I said to my mum, "look at this."

By the time the GP came—and he came to the house, on a rare and urgent home visit—an uncontrollable tremor had gripped my legs, my neck, my head, my arms.

What I remember with a needling clarity is being summoned downstairs to see the doctor. I took the stairs a step at a time. The GP, a man who had known me since I was little, stood watching, attentive, stock still, his bag in his hand, my mother beside him. Neither spoke as I came down towards them, my legs buckling under me, my hand flailing for the banister. Their faces floated in my field of vision, the swirled orange and brown hall carpet behind them, the light coming in through the opaque glass of the front door, the grey-beige of the doctor's mac, the thin gold strand of his pocket watch stretching over the front of his waistcoat.

As I reached the last stair, he turned to my mother and said: "You need to take her to hospital."

Shortly afterwards, I was lying on the examination couch of a consultant paediatrician. He asked me to grip his forefinger, as hard as I could, to follow the path of a small torch, to touch my nose with my thumb, to place my left hand on my right shoulder. He touched each of my feet and asked: "Left or right?" He smiled at me, even though I got everything wrong, and then he told my parents to drive me to the neurology department of the National Hospital in Cardiff.

Did I know the danger I was in as I sat in the back of the car, wrapped in a crocheted blanket, on my way to the big hospital, as I watched the city reel past the car windows? Now that I have children of my own, I view this scene with an altered perspective. I am aware of the panic my parents must have felt on that drive—I can taste it—and as they carried me in through the automatic doors of that hospital, as they sat in the office of the neurologist, as they watched me being admitted and wheeled away.

I have no memory of how my parents behaved, whether they let their feelings show. I was locked inside a casket of pain, of fever. I remember the neurologist's room, much larger than the kind doctor's, the toys stacked up in baskets, a particular purple dressing-gown with a fuzzy nap to it, the silver watches pinned upside-down to the nurses' chests, the way they patted my inner arm to bring up the veins, the pinch and then the sucking draw of the blood test, the cochineal shock of what appeared in the syringe. Did I sense my peril when relatives arrived, from far away, to see me, to stand beside my bed and look down on me? Or when two doctors from Great Ormond Street in London were summoned to examine me? Or during the lumbar puncture, when I was turned on to my side and held down while they drew fluid from my spinal column, the paper sheets frothing around my face as I struggled? Or the point at which I could no longer move at all, not even to gesture that I was thirsty, that my head hurt, that I needed the toilet?

Our house was a twenty-mile drive from the hospital and my parents had two other children, who needed to be fed, cared for, taken to and from school, as normal; it was term-time and my dad had to go to work. One or other of them came every day, to be with me, but there were stretches of time when I had to get used to being alone. But it was a strange, unsettling kind of alone because a nurse was stationed beside my bed, twenty-four hours a day, for whenever my parents weren't there. She fiddled with monitors and thermometers and occasionally shot out of her seat to check my pulse. Other sick children, I knew, were in the ward down the corridor. This row of rooms, faced on one side by a car park filled with late-summer sun and on the other by windows with inaccurately rendered cartoon characters, were a whole other story.

When you are a child, no one tells you that you're going to die. You have to work it out for yourself.

Clues may include: your mother crying but then pretending not to; your siblings being kept away from you; doctors looking at you with an expression of concentration, gravity and a certain fascination; nurses avoiding your eye; relatives travelling great distances to visit you. Hospital isolation rooms, invasive procedures and groups of medical students are also reliable signs.

See also: great presents.

The part of the brain that governs motor control, the cerebellum, is tucked in at the base of the skull under the cerebral hemispheres.

It does not initiate movement but plays a crucial role in its coordination, timing and precision, receiving and processing messages from the spinal cord and other sensory parts of the brain. It also has some involvement in cognitive functions, such as language and attention, as well as the regulation of fear and pleasure responses.

In appearance, it differs from the rest of the brain: it is covered with fine, parallel grooves whose texture brings to mind the throat of a blue whale. The cerebellar cortex is one continuous layer of tissue, folded into tight accordion pleats. Deep inside these folds numerous neurons are arranged in a regular formation, which give the cerebellum its enormous signal-processing abilities.

Our brains are a mass, a web, of interconnecting cells, which are lit up, like strings of fairy-lights, by communication. We are, at our very core, in our very essence, animated by circuitry, by the transmission of information.

Human brains have upwards of 100 billion nerve cells, or neurons. These, if looked at via a powerful microscope, resemble nothing so much as a tree, with a trunk (the axon) branching out into numerous filaments (the dendrites). The axon trunk of one neuron fits between the branch dendrites of its neighbour; the gap between is called a synapse. Neurons zap messages to each other at lightning speed across these gaps or synapses via minuscule electrical currents. Every single thing we do or say or react to is a result of neurons passing along electricity. If these neuron cells fail to communicate, if the electrical currents between axon and dendrite stop working, if the synapses don't conduct, for whatever reason—injury, illness, age, a stroke, a virus—your body does nothing. It falls silent, it comes to a stop, like a clockwork toy that has wound down.

Damage to neurons, axons, dendrites and synapses in the cerebellum results in disorders in fine and gross movement, motor learning, eye movements, balance, posture, speaking, reflexes, an inability to judge distances and to know when to stop. Long-term effects of cerebellar damage may also include oversensitivity, impulsiveness, irritability, ruminative and obsessive behaviours, deregulated responses to fear, sensory deficits or acuities, disinhibition, dysphoria (a profound state of unease or dissatisfaction), sleep disturbances, migraines, visuospatial disorganisation, tactile defensiveness, sensory overload, and illogical thought.

The word "cerebellum" is Latin for "little brain."

Because I am only eight, and not much spoken to by doctors—beyond them asking me, do you feel that? Can you do this? Are you able to follow the path of this torch?—I must develop new methods of interpretation. I am aware that there is a great deal being said outside in the corridor, along phone lines, behind closed doors, in the scribbled notes at the foot of my bed. I become instead a listener, a witness. I glance from the faces of my parents, standing on one side of my bed, to those of the doctors, standing on the other. I learn to be alert to nuance, to inflexions of brows, to minute alterations in facial expressions, to the setting together of teeth, the gripping of fists, to my parents' effortful, watery smiles. I search for meaning in the gaps between words, between questions, in the hesitations before the doctors' answers, in the way they all look down at me before moving towards the door and talking outside the window.

I gather, from all the listening in, that I am to have what is called a CAT-scan. The name of it is a comfort to me, conveying as it does fur, paws, whiskers, a long and curled tail. It will, from what I can glean, take photographs of my brain and these will tell the doctors how to make me better. I like the sound of this CAT-scan: the photographs, some manner of feline involvement, the making-better.

When the day finally comes, I am taken on a great trek through the hospital. I am pushed in a wheelchair by the orderly I like, the one with curling yellow hair and tales about her budgies. We travel along corridors and through doors, up and down in lifts, the paediatric wards left far behind. We are in the main hospital where grown-ups sit in chairs, where automatic doors swish open and closed, letting in jets of outside air, where people stare at me, then look quickly away. I haven't seen myself in the mirror for a long time but I get the sense, as I'm wheeled along, that I no longer look the way I used to.

And now I'm being lifted from the wheelchair onto a gurney and everybody is leaving the room—the radiologist, the orderly, the porters. Everyone.

I think I call out at this point, say, where are you, but my words are lost because the gurney seems to be moving. And I, too, am moving. There is an electronic whine and I am being slid inside the dark mouth of a large grey machine.

My head, my shoulders, my chest are inside. I am

encased in a narrow grey tube. My hips, my legs. I am being swallowed by a monster; I am trapped; I am in its gullet and I will never get out.

Then a noise starts up, a deafening, mechanised roar. I am in the eye of its storm, imprisoned by shining grey plastic.

I scream, of course. Who wouldn't? The scream doesn't register as sound, though, because the noise of the CAT-scanner is so great.

I recall the urge—stronger at this point than any other—to struggle, to fight, to move, to kick my way out of that tunnel and off that gurney and to run, out of that room, down the corridor and through those automatic doors. But I can't. I can't move. My limbs don't obey my brain, my synapses, my neuro-muscular signals. My brain isn't speaking to my muscles. They have fallen out. They ignore each other, they turn away—they pretend the other isn't there.

I must have moved a bit, however, in my panic, because all the people come back into the room. They haul me out. The orderly holds my hand as they discuss over me what to do.

Restraints are the answer. At age eight, I don't know what restraints are but, moments later, straps are tightened over my legs, my middle, my shoulders, my forehead.

This time I am screaming before my head is even in the tunnel.

The orderly with the yellow hair returns. She explains to me that I need to be still in order for the pictures of my brain to be taken. I sniff, clutching her hand. I understand, I say. Yes, I understand.

But it's no good. As soon as I sense the tunnel approach, I cannot countenance it. The idea of lying inside that close, grey, airless space is too much.

Again, I am hauled out. More discussions. The radiologist looks at his watch. The orderly is dispatched to fetch someone. Porters mill around me but no one loosens the restraints.

Please, I sob, please take them off. The pressure of the straps on my head, on my chest, is unbearable. I can feel it now, as I write this. I become, in this strange room filled with people I have never met, what my mother calls "beside myself." I wail in a voice that is hoarse, unrecognisable; panic pounds me, like sea on a harbour wall. My heart races, trips and races again. It feels like the end of everything. The people in the room shift uneasily, fiddle with charts, with blinds. They are not used to dealing with children, especially distressed ones. They are radiologists, machine operators, graph producers, results analysers. They have no idea what to do. They edge away, to the corners of the room, clearing a space around me. Tears run from my eyes down the side of my face and collect in my hair.

The orderly hurries in. She has a nurse with her. She exclaims, she mutters soothing noises, she pats my shoulder. She doesn't look me in the eyes when she says that everything is going to be fine so I don't believe her. And, as it turns out, I am right not to.

The older nurse is inverting a syringe, filling it with a clear fluid. How did I know to fear it?

"No!" I scream, filled with a new, nameless terror. "No, no, no!"

I tell them I'll be good, I promise I'll lie still. They inject me anyway.

Sedation is, I discover, only skin-deep. It covers you in a hot, suffocating rush, as if you're being swaddled, tightly, in a thick blanket. It makes you unable to speak, to articulate, to communicate. Your tongue lolls behind your teeth; your eyes look out from deep inside your skull. Sensation departs from your limbs, from the outer inches of your body.

But inside? Inside, the panic and fear still swarm, just in a smaller space.

I am rolled into the CAT-scan. The whole length of me lies encased in the grey coffin, its roof inches from my unmoving face. The machine rotates and grinds about me. I am shunted forwards, I am shunted backwards.

When I emerge, the orderly is waiting for me. She lifts me into my wheelchair; the nurse helps her as my body has lost all tension. It slumps like a corpse, heavy, unwieldy. As she settles me into the chair, tucking a blanket around me, I see that she is crying, her face scored with wet trails.

The CAT scan results are inconclusive. I am given a second the following week. This time my mother comes with me. She is allowed to stand in the room, donning a huge, elephantine robe to protect her from the radiation. She holds on to my foot while I am inside the machine. The results are, once again, inconclusive.

A year or two ago, my mother gave me, among other things, a buff envelope labelled M'S CERTIFICATES. It had been in her attic, stored in a box of stray, forgotten possessions and I didn't bother opening it for a while: its worn corners and brittle sticky tape exuded no urgency. When I did look inside, I found my O-grade and Higher results, piano exam certificates, a piece of paper telling anyone who might be interested that I had completed a level-two module in touch typing, a document attesting second prize in the poetry section of the school *eisteddfod*.

Interleaved with these testaments to accomplishments, to the hours and hours I spent practising at the piano, I also found a letter I had never seen before. It was headed in the dragon-red insignia of a hospital in Wales and was addressed "To whom it may concern" and was written by the consultant who had overseen my initial hospitalisation and then, months later, my gradual, inching recovery.

I remember him as a genial man, with wiry ginger hair, a dry and careful touch, a row of pens in his pocket, an astute gaze. He was calm with my parents, with me. He would, on occasion, lapse into Welsh and call me "*cariad*"—"love." I had monthly appointments with him for years, until I moved away from Wales, at age thirteen. I would sit on the edge of his couch and we would chat and he would tap at my knees to see if my reflexes were still inhibited, if they still swung from side to side instead of back and forth—they always did, and still do. He would ask me how school was and I would shrug, and he would glance at me without saying anything. He would bring in a group of student doctors, line them up, display my best moves to them (my pendular reflex trick, my inability to touch my finger to my nose, my unreadable handwriting, my lack of balance), then ask them what had happened to me. I felt sorry for these nervous youths as they glanced from me to him, fiddling with their shiny stethoscopes, and I was often tempted to mouth "cerebellar damage" at them, or "ataxia," just to help them along.

It is his signature at the bottom of the yellowed letter, written on a typewriter, which details the skeleton outline of what happened to me. I wonder, as I study the letter, for whom it was intended. Who, exactly, would be interested in such details, the dates and phases of my illness? Who were the people concerned? Was it for me, as an adult, an account of what had happened to me, unadorned, unembellished, from its actual time? Was it for other medics, specialists, doctors I might come across later in life who might wonder why I can't walk in a straight line or balance on one foot or orient myself among objects?

There is always a moment when I encounter someone in the medical profession—a physiotherapist, a midwife, a fertility specialist, a practice nurse, an osteopath, an optician, an anaesthetist—when they will be examining whatever part of me is relevant and an expression of puzzlement will cross their faces. They might lift a limb and flex it wonderingly back and forth; they will puzzle over why the reading glasses they have prescribed for me make me stagger and lose balance; they will not believe me when I say that I consume zero units of alcohol per week. Something about me will seem unusual, off, inexplicable, and they will glance at my notes, then back at me.

I have to clear my throat and take a deep breath.

"The thing is . . ." I begin, and then I relate to them, in brief, in essence, the contents of this letter.

Writing about this is hard, not in the sense that it is a difficult time for me to revisit. It's not that it's unwieldy or painful material to think about or mould into sentences and paragraphs. It's more that the time I spent in hospital is the hinge on which my childhood swung. Until that morning I woke up with a headache, I was one person, and after it, I was quite another. No more bolting along pavements for me, no more running away from home, no more running at all. I could never go back to the self I was before and I have no sense of who I might have been if I hadn't contracted encephalitis as a young child.

The experiences you live through while gravely ill take on a near-mystical quality. Fever, pain, medicine, immobility: all these things give you both clarity and also distance, depending on which is riding in the ascendant.

I recall my encephalitis, in its most acute phase, in flashes, in staccato bursts, in isolated scenes. Some things are as raw and immediate as the moment they happened; these, I can inhabit as myself, in the first person, in the present tense, if you like. Others I have almost to force myself to confront and I watch them as I might a film:

there is a child in a hospital bed, in a wheelchair, on an operating table; there is a child who cannot move. How can that child ever have been me?

Of its aftermath, the rehabilitation, I have a stronger sense. The coming home from hospital, the weeks and months of being at home, in bed, drifting up and down on currents of sleep, listening in on the conversations, meals, emotions, arrivals and departures of family life below. The visitors who came, bearing books and soft-toy animals and, once, a man from over the road bringing a basket of baby guinea pigs, which he let loose in my bed, their tiny, clawed, panicked pink feet skittering up and down my wasted legs.

Convalescence is a strange, removed state. Hours, days, whole weeks can slide by without your participation. You, as the convalescent, are swaddled in quiet and immobility. You are the only still thing in the house, caught in stasis, a fly in amber. You lie there on your bed like a draped stone effigy on a tomb. As the only sound you hear is that of your own body, its minutiae assumes great import, becomes magnified: the throb of your pulse, the rasp of hair shaft against the cotton weave of your pillow, the shifting of your limbs beneath the weight of blankets, the watery occlusion when eyelid meets eyelid, the sylvan susurration of air leaving and entering your mouth. The mattress presses up from underneath, bearing you aloft. The drink of water waits beside your bed, tiny silvered bubbles pressing their faces to the glass. Distances that used to appear minor—from your bed to the door, the stretch of landing to the loo, the dressing-table to the window—now take on great, immeasurable length. Outside the walls, the day turns from morning to lunchtime to afternoon to evening, then back again.

Later, I could be carried downstairs, where I might lie on the sofa, under a blanket, watching the birds swoop from leafless tree to bird-feeder. It was hard to stay warm that winter: body heat is so dependent on movement and I was unable to generate either, my fingers curled into themselves, inanimate and blue.

There were exercises and stretches that had to be performed, to keep my muscles and tendons from atrophying. My father would wrap a glass bottle in a blanket, arrange my legs over it and tell me to lift my ankles, pounding the floor if I managed to produce a minor movement. A man much wedded to statistics and research, he kept graphs of my progress. These he still has, records and results, in fading green ink, numbers of millimetres, weight in grams, ankle, knee, arm and thigh. He has a sheaf of my efforts to relearn handwriting, which range from spidery, illegible runes to shakily recognisable letters.

Mostly, though, my sisters were at school and my father at work, so it was just my mother and me in all these empty rooms. There was hydrotherapy at a pool, where I was encouraged, again and again, to lift my foot on to a submerged step, in the hope that the surrounding water would offer the support my wasted limbs needed. There were endless sessions of physiotherapy at the local hospital. I was the only child in Physiotherapy Outpatients in 1981, and I loved it: the physiotherapists seemed delighted to see me each day, as were the old ladies having their arthritic fingers coated in white wax, the elderly men recovering from strokes, squeezing rubber balls in weakened hands, lifting ankles weighted down with kilogram beanbags. There you are, they used to exclaim, as my mother pushed me over the lino, as if my appearance was all they had been waiting for.

One day, a young man with a close-cut dark beard and zippered top wheeled himself over to me when my physiotherapist had stepped away to take a phone call.

"Want one?" he said to me, dangling a gold-wrapped toffee in the air above me. He had an undulating, smooth-vowelled Valleys accent.

I said yes. He knew to unwrap it for me and he did it with an air of unconcern, seemingly not noticing the compulsive shake of my hands as I tried to take it from him.

He unwrapped another for himself. We sucked and chewed companionably for a moment, me on the floor, him in his wheelchair.

"Were you always like this, then?" he said abruptly, nodding down at me.

"No," I said, shifting the toffee from one cheek to the other. "I had a virus."

I eyed his legs, emaciated and twisted, strapped down to the footrests of his chair. They looked like mine: limbs without muscle, without tone, pared back to skin and bone. His torso, his chest and shoulders, were powerful, incongruously enormous. He was, I decided, merman in shape: human on top, tapering away to a finned, fishy tail.

"What happened to you?" I asked.

"Came off my motorbike, didn't I?" he said, crumpling his toffee wrapper. "Broke my back. Severed my spine. Don't ever," he told me, wagging a finger at me, "get on a motorbike. If you're ever tempted, think of me."

We regarded each other and I had the sense that we were both trying to see the people we had been, those ghost selves who no longer existed, those able-bodied bipeds who never thought twice about the miracle of independent movement, who had been swallowed inside the sessile, atrophied beings we now were. I looked at him and pictured a man in motorbike leathers, powering away from a village in the Valleys, his beard and black hair hidden underneath a helmet, taking a corner at an angle, parting the air with speed. Did he see a girl blurred by motion, running, bolting, scaling the branches of a tree, or leaping into the sea?

I took his advice about motorbikes, as it turned out. I have never been on one, despite the exhortations of a petrol-head boyfriend.

I don't recall the name of the bearded man from the Valleys. I knew it once: he and I saw each other most weeks. He used to say, how come you're still lying there on the floor? Time you got up, lazybones. He flirted with the physiotherapists, and called all the old ladies "darling," making them blush and laugh. He made a bet with me as to which of us would be able to take a step first. I see now, of course, that it was a ruse, that he was never going to walk again, that he wanted me to get up on my feet, in the full knowledge that he never would, perhaps because he never would.

A black-and-white film exists somewhere, maybe in the archives of a South Wales hospital, of me, age nine or ten, dressed in the kind of velour suit normally sported by inmates of Florida retirement homes, attempting, with varying degrees of success, to walk along a ward, to climb some stairs, to wield a pen. I look around at the camera and smile, as if I'm appearing in a holiday film, not medical-research footage. There is another, a few years later, where I am lankier, more sullen, more reluctant, wearing drainpipe jeans and a shapeless woollen sweater pulled down over my hands. There are probably doctors, paediatricians, neurologists, physiotherapists out there who were shown these films during their training to teach them about cerebellar disorders.

Physiotherapy Outpatients, the staff and the patients I met there, are the reason I am ambulatory today. That they didn't give up on me, that they believed I was capable of movement, of motion, of recovery, when the doctors didn't, meant that I walked. If someone says you can do something, if you can see they really believe it, it puts that possibility within your grasp. "Come on," I remember the bearded man calling, as I struggled to lift my knees from the mat.

"You can do it," nodded the old ladies from their place at the wax machine.

"Give me your hand," said the physiotherapist. "I won't let you fall."

It also lulled me into a false sense of how accepted and wanted I would be, as a child who could barely walk, barely hold a pen, had lost the ability to run, ride a bike, catch a ball, feed herself, swim, climb stairs, hop, skip, a child who travelled everywhere in a humiliating outsized buggy. I was loved there, I was special, I was accepted, I was cheered on: everyone there wanted only the best for me. It gave me no preparation, no sense of what was waiting for me when I eventually went back to school, where people would call me a *spaz*, a *moron*, a *joey*, would demand to know what was wrong with me or what they would catch from me. Where people would trip me up just for a laugh, would spit on me and pull my hair, tell me I was *diseased*, a *retard*. Where the education authorities agreed to move my classroom downstairs but not the lunch rooms, so every day I had the choice of either going without lunch or climbing the stairs the only way I could, on all fours, like a bear, like a baby, with the whole school watching.

We do what we have to do to survive; as a species, we are inventive in the face of adversity. Robert Frost said, "The best way out is always through," and I believe this to be true but, at the same time, if you can't go through, you can always go around.

I ate a lot of packed lunches in the downstairs toilets, with the door locked, my feet tucked up so no one could locate me. The smell of bleach, of a certain type of paper towel, always takes me back to this: misshapen peanut-butter sandwiches, eaten alone, cross-legged on a cistern.

The illness comes in and out of focus for me, in adulthood. I can go for days without thinking about it; at other times it feels like a defining event. It means nothing, it means everything.

It means I have to scrawl succinct yet numerous sentences into those too-small spaces on forms that ask, "Any other medical history?" It has meant I need to explain certain things to people I spend time with: why I might fall over or persistently drop cutlery or knock over mugs, why I can't walk or cycle long distances, why I need to do a series of exercises and stretches several times a day.

It means that my perception of the world is altered, unstable. I see things that aren't there: lights, flashes, spots or rents in the fabric of vision. Some days, holes will crackle and burn in the centre of whatever I look at, and text disappears the minute I turn my gaze upon it. The floor may lurch, like the deck of a ship. I can turn my head towards a noise and my brain will confidently and suddenly inform me that, instead of standing up, I am lying down, that the room is the wrong way up, that everything is not as it looks. I can turn over in bed and somehow my cerebellum won't keep up and will be left facing the other way; I have to close my eyes, press my fists to my face, breathe deeply until my brain decides to catch up with me. My two-year-old child can knock me over with very little effort.

"Is it just me," I will ask my husband, "or is this sofa tilting sideways?"

"It's just you," he will answer patiently.

"And the ceiling isn't shaking either?"

"No," he will say, turning a page of his book, "it isn't."

It means that my life has involved, for almost as long as I remember, a series of cover-ups, smoke-screens, sleights of hand. I sleep with a light on so that I don't fall if I have to get out of bed at night. I don't drink alcohol or take drugs, never have and never will because I cannot touch anything that might affect my already shaky motor control. I stammered appallingly for most of my childhood and adolescence; I still do, on occasion, when confronted with a hostile voice, a sceptical stare or the bald head of a radio microphone.

I fall or stumble if I don't concentrate. When I ascend or descend stairs, I have to look down at my feet and apply myself to the task of meeting each tread. Don't ever talk to me when I'm climbing stairs or negotiating a doorway: these acts require my full attention.

I will never play Blind Man's Buff or surf or wear high-heels or bounce on a trampoline. Tables crowded with cutlery, water glasses, jugs, vases, napkins present me with huge problems. I sit down at them with a sense of dread, eyeing them as you might a particularly challenging exam paper, with a mixture of fear, anxiety and incipient humiliation. It is a sensory, spatial overload that can result in spilt water, dropped forks, broken glass and peculiar, disorienting inroads into my vestibular sense: too many objects, too many demands on my faulty senses, too many things to navigate.

I carry a lot of bruises, blackish-purple leopard spots down my legs and sides, from encounters with bookcases, door jambs, table corners, chair legs. I dread book-festival stages with steps—to fall, in front of an audience!—but I refuse, absolutely, to accept assistance. When I carry babies, especially new ones, on stairs, I do it like my primate ancestors, employing my spare hand as extra ballast.

My left arm is pretty useless: it can just about hold a bag of shopping or the hand of a child or steer a bike or a buggy, but anything more than that is too much. I was in a Chinese restaurant with my friend recently: I lifted the teapot with my left hand to pour her a drink and missed her cup by about five inches. Scalding dark liquid shot out over the table, over our food, our chopsticks, our napkins, causing us both to dissolve into inappropriate laughter.

"Sorry," I got out. "My left hand isn't much use."

"I see that," she replied, mopping herself down. "Maybe you should just sell it."

"Maybe I will," I said. "For sale. One useless hand."

It also means I have a powerful aversion to small, enclosed spaces.

When my first child began to walk, I took him to a soft-play centre near where we were living, in London. I had never been to such a place. It was an enormous edifice, several storeys high, made up of cushioned planes and steps, spiralling slides, pits filled with brightly coloured balls. How he loved to run in his drunken-sailor gait along its corridors, to climb the stairs, to dive face-first into the balls.

On the highest level, he was ahead of me as we ran along a neon-bright padded floor and then he vanished into a narrow blue tunnel, speed-crawling into its shiny plastic mouth. I was just able to see his socked feet disappear.

I crouched by the tunnel's mouth; I called his name. "Come back," I said.

He laughed, by way of reply.

I straightened up. I assessed the play structure. Was

there any other way to get to where he was without using the plastic tunnel?

No.

I crouched down again. The tunnel was probably the width of three hand spans—I would have to squeeze myself in, possibly wriggle like a snake. And it was long, longer than my body. It would take several seconds for me to reach the other side.

There was my son, framed by the tunnel's exit, like a creature seen at the wrong end of a telescope, and he was beckoning, saying, come, come.

Is it terrible to admit that I still hesitated? I couldn't, in that moment, think of anything I would rather do less than enter that narrow plastic space, submit myself to its confines.

I did, of course. Maternal love is a great force, greater perhaps than all others.

When I got to the other side, I was shaking, stricken. My son patted me on the cheek and muttered what I said when I wanted to reassure him: "'S aright. 'S aright." It's all right.

Coming so close to death as a young child, only to resurface again into life, imbued in me for a long time a brand of recklessness, a cavalier or even crazed attitude to risk.

It could, I can see, have gone the other way, and made me into a person hindered by fear, hobbled by caution. Instead, I leapt off harbour walls. I walked alone in remote mountains. I took night trains through Europe on my own, arriving in capital cities in the middle of the night with nowhere to stay. I cycled blithely along what is dubbed "South America's Most Dangerous Road," a vertiginous, crumbling, eroding track cut into a steep peak, the verge of which is liberally punctuated by shrines to those who have fallen to their deaths. I walked across frozen lakes. I swam in dangerous waters, both metaphorically and literally.

It was not so much that I didn't value my existence but more that I had an insatiable desire to push myself to embrace all that it could offer. Nearly losing my life at the age of eight made me sanguine—perhaps to a fault—about death. I knew it would happen, at some point, and the idea didn't scare me; its proximity felt instead almost familiar. The knowledge that I was lucky to be alive, that it could so easily have been otherwise, skewed my thinking. I viewed my continuing life as an extra, a bonus, a boon: I could do with it what I wanted. And not only had I tricked death but I had escaped a fate of incapacity. What else was I going to do with my independence, my ambulatory state, except exploit it for all it was worth?

A teacher at school gave us John Donne's Sonnet X to study, and the poet's depiction of Death as an arrogant, ineffectual, conceited despot made me smile in recognition:

Death, be not proud, though some have called thee
Mighty and dreadful, for thou art not so . . .
. . . nor yet canst thou kill me.

This insouciance stopped the minute I had children, when suddenly I worried that my two-fingered taunts to Death might come back to bite me. What if Donne's proud, vengeful personification of Death decided to return and seek recompense for all my insolence? What if it took me, took my baby? When you engender a life, you open yourself to risk, to fear. Holding my child, I realised my vulnerability to death: I was frightened of it, for the first time. I knew all too well how fine a membrane separates us from that place, and how easily it can be perforated.

When I told a boyfriend a shortened version of what happened to me as a child—more in the spirit of explanation than anything else—he looked appalled, as people mostly do, and said, "You were so *unlucky*."

I remember feeling surprised because unlucky is the

opposite of how I view it. They thought I would die; I didn't. They thought I wouldn't walk or swim or hold a pencil again; I did. They thought I would need a wheelchair for the rest of my life; the wheelchair was returned to the NHS after a year or so. They thought I would need to attend a special school; I didn't. They envisaged for me a life of limitations, institutions, incapability, dependency.

I consider myself steeped in luck, in good fortune to have avoided the fate the doctors decreed for me. I have been showered with shamrocks, my pockets filled with rabbits' feet, found the crock of gold at the end of every rainbow. I could not have asked for more from life, to have been spared what might have been. I could have died there in that hospital but I didn't. I could have been condemned to a life of immobility but I wasn't. I dodged a bullet—many, in fact.

I surfaced one day in hospital to find a man leaning over my bed. He had wide-spaced, staring eyes, a heavy gold chain around his neck, not dissimilar to the one our neighbours' Labrador wore, and wispy whitish hair standing out around his head. He was familiar and strange, all at the same time.

"Hello, hello," he said, "what have we here?"

As soon as he spoke, I realised that I knew him from the television. Children would write to him with their wildest wishes—to fly an aeroplane, to look after the elephants at the zoo, to tap-dance on stage—and he, like a genie, would grant them.

And now here he was, at my bedside. He stared down at me, with a piercing, assessing, slightly haughty gaze; I stared back in bafflement, astonishment.

Years later, I will be in a traffic jam, waiting in line for a red light to change, my children in the back of the car, and the news comes on the radio. The headline item is that this man's numerous paediatric hospital visits were not what they seemed. I will sit with my hands resting on the steering wheel, staring through the rain-flecked windscreen. I am shocked and yet not shocked at all. I recall the moment he turned to the nurse and said, "You can go. I'll look after her." The nurse shook her head and stayed.

I listen to the newsreader for a moment, then jab at the radio, to silence it. I don't want my children to hear, don't want those words to spiral into their uncomprehending ears. Later that evening, I will call my mother and remind her that he came to see me.

She will take a sharp breath and say quickly: "Where was I?"

"I don't know," I will say. "You weren't there. But it's okay. He didn't lay a finger on me."

"Are you sure?"

"I'm sure. The nurse wouldn't leave. She stayed with me the whole time."

That background figure in a white dress and hat, moving about the room behind this man with his tracksuit and his bracelets and his loud voice and his questions about how I was feeling and when I would be up and about again, and how about that lovely photo on the bedside cabinet of me in my ballet leotard?

She never left the room. She shook her head when he suggested, again, that she leave, that she take a break. I was on twenty-four-hour watch, she explained. I remember her as young, sweet-faced, with a brown bun, happy to read stories to me for hours. She stayed there, hovering behind him, refusing to abandon her post: another saviour, another seraph in disguise.

Before he left, the man gave me a book, signed by him. He tucked it in between the mattress and the metal bars around the bed. It was about making your own Hallowe'en costumes. My mother read it to me the following day, when she came to visit. Together, we looked at the diagrams and illustrations and talked about what we would make when I was better. I kept it for years, that book; I followed the instructions to make a severed head out of papier-mâché, covering a balloon in strips of newspaper and leaving it to dry in the airing cupboard.

Recently, going through a box of my old books to find something to read to my children, I came across the book again. I pulled it out, opened it, looked at his signature. Then I crossed the room and jammed it into the heart of the wood-stove. It burnt quickly, ferociously, leaving behind a ghost of its shape in black, flaking ash.

It is the strangest sensation, not being able to move. It is not a heavy feeling, as you might imagine, but light. You inhabit your being as you might a house: the body is a structure within which you must live, as best you can, flitting from one wall to the next. The framework is inert but you—that invisible, interior part of yourself—are anything but. Your skin registers heat, cold, the crease in a bedsheet, the weight of a blanket, the rasp of a night-dress label but it is nothing to do with you. Not any more.

What to do, when you cannot move, when you are bedridden? How to occupy, divert and distract yourself? I spend a long time staring at the ceiling above me, the clock on the wall, the rubber seal that runs around the door. I memorise each and every detail of the room, the way the paint on the far wall is a slightly paler shade of cream than it is on the others, the strip lighting that glows yellow at the edges and white in the centre, the way the tap drips, once-twice, in quick succession and then not for ages. I gaze out of the window, watching the sunlight thrown from car windscreens to skitter on my ceiling. I absorb the strange snippets of conversation, released like soap bubbles into my room as people flit past my windows. I am given to begging anyone who comes near to read to me. My mother spends hours narrating the tales of the Brothers Grimm, a book of Bible stories; my father favours a compendium of Irish folktales. I lie there and consider Moses afloat on a river, coming to rest in a bank of reeds, David selecting the perfect stone with which to load his slingshot, Finn McCool's clever wife, Oonagh, breaking the teeth of a rival giant with an iron griddle, hidden in a loaf of bread.

Eventually, a neighbour lends a selection of story tapes: never have I seen such things before. A solution at last. A tape-player is set up beside my bed and I can listen to Felicity Kendal reading *My Naughty Little Sister* and a rather sonorous male voice intoning the tales of Beatrix Potter.

Lettuce has a *soporific effect*.

He wore his *galoshes*.

Jemima was a *simpleton*.

But neither of them made any remark.

I roll these words around my head like pebbles; I repeat them to myself. I tuck them away.

I listen to the tapes over and over again, often at night-time, when the hospital is filled with that curious humming almost-quiet, when the nurses' shoes squeal on the floors, when the dark from outside reaches in through the slits in the blinds, when the hands on the clock opposite my bed leap and stop, leap and stop. The bad part is when the tape finishes and clicks off with a mechanical *thunk* and I must wait until someone comes to turn it over for me. The awfulness of the silence then, its crushing, rushing stillness.

On such a night, I am awake. My watching nurse has said that, no, I cannot listen to another side of a tape: I must sleep, she says, I need to rest.

My headache pulses away, a bright, daemonic metronome. I look out, always, from behind its blinding white mask. The noise of the television from the ward has ceased, so I know it is late; it is deep into the night. Am I falling into sleep or something else when I hear the noise in the corridor outside?

Footsteps, the fluting voice of a child, a rhythmic noise like a toy being dragged along the lino.

The child says something in a high, enquiring tone, and the nurse tells him to be quiet.

"Hush," she says. "There's a little girl dying in there."

I inserted a scene like this into my third novel. I recast it, reimagined it, repositioned it. It was the only time—until this—that I ever put anything to do with my encephalitis into writing. I made the girl in the bed into the sister of the protagonist; I made the child outside into a little boy, pulling a toy train. I made the nurse beside me jump up, embarrassed and shocked, to shut the door. I used to read it whenever I did public events for the book, which strikes me now as an odd choice. Why did I do that? Why read a scene drawn from what is possibly one of the worst moments you could ever live through—a child, learning they are dying?

Like Nina in my novel, I did think for a moment about the dying girl, how old she might be, how old you had to be to die. I felt sorry for her and I looked over at the nurse, to see if she was sorry too.

The truth is I never saw the child making a noise out there in the corridor, or the nurse who ought to have known better, who needed to learn to keep her voice down. I couldn't turn my head to see.

The truth is the nurse beside me didn't leap up to shut the door. She looked confused and then she blushed, as if caught out in a lie, a red tide rising up from her collar. She looked annoyed, like someone who had just been told they had to do overtime. She shuffled over to the door and flicked at it with her heel so that the handle almost caught but didn't quite.

In the novel, the scene ends here, with Nina realising that the child they are discussing, the child who is dying, is her, but life, of course, is different. It carries on. No one yells, "CUT!" No one puts in a full stop and leaves the chapter neatly there.

So in real life the door swung open again, and I heard the unseen child and nurse proceed to discuss my imminent demise. When might it occur? Soon—tomorrow, the day after, some time this week, I learnt. Why was it happening? I was very ill. Why couldn't the doctors make me better? My illness was too serious. Did that mean I was never going home? No, I was never going home. Was I going to Heaven? Yes, came the answer, in a didactic tone, because I had been a good girl and had taken all my medicine.

DAUGHTER

The present day

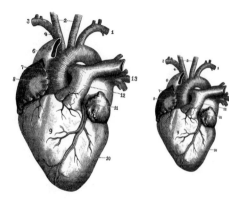

We are racing in a car through lush and verdant countryside, the roads hair-pinning around field boundaries, when I realise that my daughter's life is in danger.

The landscape outside the car is that of a Renaissance painting: rolling green hills layering and repeating until they disappear into a blue haze. It is Palm Sunday. Earlier in the day, we went past a church and the people coming out of Mass were all clutching olive branches. The sun is so high in the sky that the trees and barns at the sides of the road stand in pools of their own shadow.

Some minutes earlier I crawled into the back of the car, the kit of emergency medication in my hands, and I am now holding my daughter as my husband drives, as fast as the car will go.

My daughter's breathing is shallow, laboured, her lips distended, her skin patched and livid. The delicate features of her face are sunken, swollen, distorted. Her hands clutch mine but her eyes are rolling back in her head. I touch her cheek, I say her name. I say, stay awake, stay with us.

In moments like these, your thinking shrinks, sharpens, narrows. The world shutters up and you are reduced to a crystalline pinpoint, to a single purpose: to keep your child alive, to ensnare her in the world of the living, to hang on to her and never let go.

At the front of your mind will be the instructions and stages of the emergency medical plans that are taped to the inside of your kitchen cupboards. These have been pored, frowned, sometimes wept over. I have had them laminated, preserved. A tiny headshot of my daughter, younger than she is now, looking at the camera with an expression of amusement and trust, is glued to the top.

In everyday life, phrases and parentheses and names of drugs from these documents will float unbidden through my thoughts. *If breathing becomes laboured,* my mind will murmur to me, as I read a story to my youngest child. *Auto-adrenalin injection,* I will hear, as I stir the porridge on a school morning, or *Call for backup. Stay with patient,* I will find myself intoning, as I wait at a red light. *At risk of a life-threatening allergic reaction.*

Right now, as I sit in the car with her, the documents are clear, in their entirety, in my head. I can see them before me, the little green boxes, filled with plainly worded text, with phone numbers, with flow-charts, the confident arrows leading from one stage of suffering to another, from one circle of Hell to the next. I have them memorised, down pat, internalised. All those times when my mind whispered extracts at me were, I see, a rehearsal. A necessary bedding down of information for times like this. Now the green boxes are playing out in front of me.

Anaphylaxis: the condition was discovered in 1901 by a French doctor called Charles Richet, who was studying the effects of jellyfish venom on dogs. He initially thought that giving them a small dose of the venom would immunise them against future doses; in fact, with the second injections, the dogs developed breathing difficulties, then dramatically died. He is reported to have shouted, *"C'est un phénomène nouveau, il faut le baptiser!"*

He originally coined the word as "aphylaxis" from the Greek: the prefix "a-" meaning "without" and "-phylaxis," "protection." Without protection. He later added the extra letters to make it the more pronounceable "anaphylaxis." The discovery won him a Nobel Prize.

The first documented case is said to be that of Menes, an Egyptian pharaoh, who died in 2641 BC after a sting from a hornet. Not such a *phénomène nouveau* after all. You can see the hieroglyphic panel, complete with lethal insect. I have pored over the depiction and cannot but imagine the scene: the darting pain of the sting, the rash up his neck, the swelling of limbs, of airways, the short-ness of breath, the collapse. How long did it take for Menes to die? Did he know what was happening to him? Had he been stung before? I hope for his sake it wasn't prolonged, that death came quickly. The horror of suffo-cating in your own body, the cruelty of your very life's blood turning against you.

My daughter, like Menes, like Richet's dogs, lives without protection. The first sign of anaphylactic shock is often hives, a reddened and raised rash around the mouth or down the limbs. The attack can sometimes be allayed at this point, with a dose of oral antihistamine, if luck is on your side, if the planets are aligned. But the lips, hands and eyes may swell, then the tongue. Breathing becomes restricted, noisy. And then you know you're on dangerous ground, that the antihistamine hasn't worked, hasn't appeased the gods: you need a jolt to the system, you need adrenalin and you need it fast. The victim will be screaming at this point, clawing at their throat, hoarse with panic and fear. They may then go white and limp. They may lose consciousness. If untreated, as Menes would have been, cardiac arrest isn't far behind.

On average, my daughter suffers allergic reactions, with varying degrees of severity, around twelve to fifteen times a year: I keep a detailed record. She was born with an immunology disorder, which means that her immune system underreacts to some things and overreacts to others. Whereas my other children might get a cold, she will be knocked sideways, requiring hospitalisation, a ventilator and a drip. If she encounters anything on the long list of things to which she is allergic, she may go into anaphylactic shock. This can happen if she eats something with a trace of a nut. Or if she sits at a table where someone has recently consumed sesame seeds. Or if an egg is cracked nearby. Or if she is stung by a bee or a wasp. If she touches the hand of someone who has been eating nuts or eggs or salad with pumpkin oil. If she enters a cloakroom and one of the coats has a peanut in its pocket. If she sits in a paddling pool with someone wearing sun-cream containing almond oil. If a café tells me there is no nut or egg in that biscuit, but they pick it up with tongs used earlier for a brownie. If someone across the train carriage or plane aisle opens the wrapping of an energy bar with nuts. If the person next to her at school has eaten muesli for breakfast.

I could go on.

We live, then, in a state of high alert. I have to know where she is and who she is with at all times. I enter a room and scan it like a SWAT team: What in here could pose a danger to her? The table surface, the door handles, the soft furnishings, that crumb-strewn plate? Her teachers and classroom assistants have to be trained in allergies, in medication, in resuscitation. I read and reread ingredient and allergy lists. I check and recheck with people wherever we go: are you sure, are you positive, are you certain, can you swear on your life that soup contains no nuts or seeds? Could it have been touched by a utensil recently used to stir nuts? Are you positive your hot chocolate has no powdered hazelnut? Can I please see the packaging?

We never leave the house without her medication, her emergency kit. We know how to inject her, how to administer cardio-pulmonary resuscitation, how to recognise the signs of low blood pressure, respiratory distress, urticaria, the onset of cardiac failure.

I know I must nod calmly when people tell me they understand exactly how I feel because they have a gluten allergy, which makes them really bloated whenever they eat bread. I know to be patient and genial when I have to explain that, no, it's not okay to bring that hummus into our house. No, it's not a good idea to give her a little bit to get her used to it. No, please don't open that near her. Yes, your lunch could kill my child.

I taught her brother, at the age of six, how to dial 999 and say into the receiver the sentence, "This is an emergency case of anaphylaxis." *Ana-fil-ax-iss:* he used to practise the pronunciation, to make sure he'd got it right. My life with her involves a fair amount of sprinting along hospital corridors. The nurses in our local A and E department greet her by name. Her consultant allergist has told me several times that we should never take her outside the range of a good hospital.

Our problem, in the car in Italy, is that we don't know where we are. We are lost. A friend, earlier in the day, invited us to her friends' farm: there would be donkeys, she promised, and newborn goats, puppies, fresh cheeses, horses, pigs. I rapidly ran, as I always do, through an inventory of the risks involved in such an outing: minimal, surely. We won't be eating anything, we'll be outside in the fresh air and sunshine, I can give her a low dose of antihistamine, just in case. She adores animals, and what reason could there be to deprive her of this trip? Shouldn't all children get the chance to pet some donkeys and handfeed a newborn goat?

We followed our friend's car in ours, blindly, blithely, without glancing at a map. We have spent the morning at the farm, petting the goats, with their tiny, emerging horns, stroking the donkey, watching the tortoise toil stolidly through the long grass. When my daughter began to feel itchy and ill, we left, striking out into the country-side, heading in what we thought was the right direction.

Now she is beyond feeling ill. Now she is in danger, and now we are lost.

We have the vaguest sense that we are somewhere on the Lazio border, but there is no phone signal and our satnav, on the dashboard, is spooling in space. Life is slipping from my child with every passing second. Once you use the intramuscular adrenalin, you need immediately to call an ambulance. She needs a hospital: she needs a heart monitor, a dose of steroids, blood-pressure stabilising medication, a resuscitation suite, a doctor— several, in fact.

How can we call for help if we have no phone signal and no idea where we are?

I am going over her movements in my mind, wondering what on earth it could have been, where I went wrong, what I didn't notice, what could possibly have slipped through my net of vigilance. Pollen from a nearby flow-ering nut tree, a trace of something on someone's hand, something in the animal feed? Can she have inhaled some nut or seed dust from somewhere? What was it that I failed to see, failed to prevent, failed to notice?

My eyes meet my husband's in the rear-view mirror. I try to communicate with him using no words, because I don't want to alarm her or her siblings, but I am willing him to understand this: she is dying, like Menes, right here in my arms.

Her skin is bubbling and blistering, each breath a struggling symphony of whistles and wheezes. Her face, under the scarlet hives, under the grotesque swelling, is ghastly white.

I think: she cannot die, not now, not here. I think: how could I have let this happen?

There was once a girl who met a boy and his friend in the middle of a courtyard. The girl was cross about something that day (it doesn't matter what), and as she talked to the boy and his friend, she kicked a wall with the toes of her boots. She wore big boots in those days, black ones that laced up round her ankles, and the shortest shorts the boy had ever seen.

The boy walked away, thinking he had never met anyone quite as frightening as that girl. The girl walked away, thinking the boy was very shy. Neither would have suspected that they would, many years later, fall in love and, eventually, marry.

Twelve years after the wall/boot incident, the boy and the girl—or, rather, the man and the woman—have a child. The baby has the woman's eyes and the man's peaked hairline; he is, they are both deeply and privately sure, the most beautiful baby ever born.

When the child starts to walk and talk, the woman thinks she might like another child. She becomes pregnant, but this baby dies before it even lives. She cries a lot, she hugs her child more tightly and tries to get pregnant again. She tries and waits and waits and tries but, for some reason, her body won't do what it did before. It has shut down. It seems to have forgotten how to do it, how to pull off that particular trick.

She takes vitamins; she does yoga; she goes to a practitioner who sticks very fine needles into her flesh; she waits and waits. Each month, every twenty-eight days, feels like another failure, another baffling loss.

A doctor takes some blood tests. "There is no reason you can't have another baby," he tells the woman.

Someone scans her innards. "There is no reason," they tell her, "you can't have another baby."

Then why, the woman wants to know, isn't it happening?

They can't tell her that. They shrug their shoulders, they turn away, they wash their hands. "If you stop thinking about it," they say, "it will probably just happen."

The woman stamps away across the car park. If there was a wall, she might have kicked it. This is, she decides, as she grinds her key into the ignition, her least favourite sentence in the English language.

"*If you stop thinking about it*," she snarls, at the automated barrier as it lifts to let her out, "*it will probably just happen.*"

"*If you stop thinking about it*," she snaps at the silent radio.

As she pulls up outside her son's school, she is muttering, "*It will just happen. Probably.*" She eyes the group of mothers waiting at the gate. All of them have a child in the school, perhaps two, and a smaller child in a sling or buggy. Her son has recently stopped asking when he can have a baby sister or brother; this has not gone unnoticed by the woman. He did, however, only last week, ask if it was possible to play tig on your own.

She takes a deep breath, opens the car door, tosses back her hair, and steps out.

The problem is, of course, that she cannot think about anything else. She cannot not think about it. The desire, the need, the grief, the frustration of it is ever-present. It forms a constant undertow to everything she does. She wants a baby; she wants a sibling for her son; she wants the baby she lost; she wants any baby at all. It's like wearing a pair of glasses she cannot take off.

The man and the woman go to a different doctor. This

clinic has opaque windows; the waiting room is full of still-faced people; the air here is steeped with longing, with loss, with faint hope. No one in this place will ever ask her when she is going to *get her skates on.* No one here will say the words *tick-tock, tick-tock.*

On one visit, the woman takes her son with her and the other people in the waiting room look quickly at him—at his T-bar sandals and rolled-down socks, at his shoulder-blades under his shirt, at his fingers gripping the hand of his mother—and away, and the woman feels ashamed of her own sadness, when she has so much, when she has him. These women have been coming to this place for years and have nothing to show for it. Less than nothing.

The woman injects herself, has scans, allows her blood to be screened, lies back on beds while they search and delve with metal instruments.

When she gets the call to say it hasn't worked, that the blood test has come back as negative, insufficient, that it's all been for nothing, that the embryos haven't taken, she is standing at the cheese counter in the supermarket.

Okay, she says into her phone, staring at the Cheddar, the creamy-sided Brie, the wedges of Parmesan. Okay, thank you, I understand. She hangs up without saying goodbye.

"Who was that?" Her son is gazing up at her, clutching a packet of his favourite triangle-shaped cheeses.

No one, she says. Nothing. It was no one.

It was a brand of magic. Of this I am certain.

I am not a mystical, superstitious person. I don't believe in luck, in Fate, in any deity, karmic repercussions or divine retribution. I don't cast spells.

Nevertheless, for weeks after that moment at the cheese counter, I persistently felt listless, tired, nauseated. I went to Skye, in a camper-van, where it rained and rained, not once in a while but every day, without let-up. I bled, on and on, more than seemed possible. I went into a chemist and heard myself asking, in a low mumble, for iron tablets and "sanity towels," a mispronunciation that made me collapse into hysterical laughter. As I paid, I saw the lady behind the counter eyeing me with concern.

It rained horizontally; it rained vertically; it rained in swirls. I cried up mountains, on beaches, in woodlands, in the sea: wherever it was possible to cry without my son noticing. I swam in the fairy pools at Glenbrittle, zipping myself into my wetsuit and diving through the watery arches, resurfacing into air so cold it made my lungs hurt. There would, I decided, as I thrashed through those clear, chill waters, be no more fertility treatments, no more trying; there would be no more babies in our house.

I came home and cleared out the garage: all the baby blankets, Moses baskets, maternity clothes were packed off to the charity shops. I'd had a child, and I would have no more. It was finished, that chapter of my life. It was over, it was done, and I needed to come to terms with that.

But something was wrong. My body had done its initial expulsion, after the IVF, then nothing. It seemed to be on hold or waiting for something. Ten weeks since the IVF ended, then eleven, then twelve, and still no period. So I went back to the clinic, which I of course now loathed, and saw the doctor, yet again, and he sent me for a scan—"to see what's happening"—and as they rolled the scanner over my belly, there it was. An alert, active form, limbs waving frantically, as if to attract attention, a heart that was pulsing and pulsing, turning from light to dark and back again.

The doctor gasped. The nurses covered their mouths, then began fluttering anxiously through my file. How had this happened? they asked. How had this embryo held on, despite no signs of pregnancy, despite the heavy bleeding, despite the loss of its twin, despite a negative blood test, despite all evidence that the embryos had left, departed, drifted loose?

But there she was, despite everything, thirteen weeks of gestation under her belt and waving at us for all she was worth.

My daughter was born six months later, in early spring. She was small, wide-eyed, otter-soft, with a nap of white-blonde hair covering her head. When anyone took her from me, she wailed as if her heart might break. The first night she spent curled on my shoulder, very quiet and still. Every time I looked down at her, her eyes were half open, looking back at me, as if checking I was still there, that I hadn't gone anywhere.

In any fairy-tale, getting what you wish for comes at a cost. There is always a codicil, an addendum to the granting of a wish. There is always a price to pay. How was I to know, as I held her that night, as I stared at the ultrasound screen, as I burst out of the clinic, fumbling with my phone, trying to press the right buttons so I could call my husband, the boy from the courtyard, and say, you'll never guess what I've just seen?

How I've longed that it could have been me, the wisher, who had to pay the magic's price, to bear the brunt. I would give anything to take the curse from her, to transfer it to my own shoulders. But, as it is, I must stand by while the innocent, the child, the baby must be the one to suffer.

And suffer she does.

On the second day of my second child's life, when I was still wired up to a drip-stand, woozy from anaesthetic, I removed the sleepsuit the nurses had put her in. My hands shook, with the novelty or the drugs, hard to say which, and as I eased the suit away from her there was a shower of something the consistency of snow. Suddenly my lap was dusted with white.

Odd, I thought, then tossed the sleepsuit aside and forgot all about it.

That was the first clue.

When doctors ask me when she first developed eczema, I say, she was born with it. A week later, her skin was peeling off in strips, like dried glue. The cuffs of jackets seemed too harsh for the petal delicacy of her; the circle-backs of poppers and the undersides of zips were a metallic outrage, printing her with red, raw lesions.

Her skin never looked like skin should. It was patchy, hot, sand-dry, crêpy with inflammation. By the time she was a month old, she was encased in the livid, raw body-cast of eczema. Her skin split open if she flexed her wrist, her arm, her leg; the disease had invaded every millimetre, every last crevice of her, from the joints of her toes to the innermost crease of her ears.

When people stepped up towards the pram that spring, eager to see the baby, I found I was gripping the handle, bracing myself. Please, I was silently willing them, find something nice to say: Compliment her blue eyes, her blonde curls. Don't reel back in horror. Don't gasp, what's wrong with her?

When I think back to those days, I am overcome by an urge to go up to the person I was then, put a hand on her shoulder and say: you have no idea what is coming. At that time, you see, I still thought it was something that could be sorted out. It was only eczema, wasn't it? How bad could it be?

Some things I didn't know, as I pushed her red pram up the hill: that there is no known cure for eczema. That even though her skin seemed as bad as it could possibly be, it would get an awful lot worse. That eczema, at its most severe, can be dangerous and even life-threatening. That her skin would torture her every minute of every day. That it indicated much more serious health problems for her.

By the time she was almost nine months old, she had seen the health visitor, who had referred her to a GP, who had referred her to a dermatology nurse, who had

I AM, I AM, I AM

referred her to a consultant dermatologist at the big London hospital where she and her brother were born.

On my way out of this appointment, I bumped into my friend Constance. She took one look at me, standing there on a pavement, and asked what on earth was wrong. I sat down on a low wall, holding on to my daughter, who was scratching and writhing and bleeding into her clothing, and wept. Constance took the baby while I told her how we had waited forty-five minutes to see the consultant, and when we walked in she was already writing something on a pad. I had assumed it was some notes for her preceding patient, but then the doctor had ripped a sheet off her prescription pad with a flourish and handed it to me before I'd even sat down. "There!" she'd said. "The good news is that, at this age, they haven't learnt to scratch!" She didn't examine my daughter; she didn't ask me a single question; she didn't even glance into the pram. If she had, she might have seen my tiny child sandpapering her wrists against the straps of her harness, she might have seen a baby covered from crown to foot in open, weeping abrasions, she might have seen the desperate, weary, tortured look in my daughter's eyes—a look no nine-month-old should ever have.

As I'd taken the lift down to street-level, I'd glanced at the prescription and had seen that it was for the very same paraffin-based emollient the health visitor had given me when my daughter was five weeks old. It had made absolutely no difference.

When I was in my twenties, still trying to find the right path in life, I used to have a particularly vivid recurring dream. It came in phases, this dream, but always with the same scenario, the same setting, and usually at a time of flux or upheaval. It would make an appearance, rising from my subconscious, if I was moving, yet again, from one dodgy and damp flat to another, if I had a new job, if I'd left a man or if a man had left me, if I'd received some awful news, if something bad had happened to someone I loved. Always at these moments the dream would resurface, often for several nights in a row.

In the dream, I would be walking along a track and ahead of me would be a child, a girl with fair, curling hair. Always, she was crying. I could see that her thin shoulders were bent in distress, her hands wiping at her tears, her feet stumbling as she walked.

I would always attempt to catch up with her. Sometimes this was allowed to happen; at others, I tried and tried to reach her but the distance between us only increased. If I managed to get near her, I would lift her up and carry her, sometimes on my back. I can still recall the dream-sensation of her arms gripping my shoulders.

For such a little child, she was heavy, as if her suffering weighed down on both of us. If I managed to reach her, if I took her into my arms, she would stop crying: I was always aware of my ability to bring about this change. Sometimes I would jerk awake, suffused with panic, knowing I hadn't been able to help.

The first time I ever had this dream was in the middle of the night on the Trans-Siberian Railway, as I was wending my way back from China, age twenty-two. I remember waking with a jolt, sitting up in my bunk, clutching my sleeping-bag around me and looking about the compartment, as if the child might be standing there, waiting for me.

She wasn't.

I climbed down from my bunk, tiptoed past my cabin-mates, who were sleeping below me, and out into the corridor. The train was swaying and clanking through the night, pulling us north as we slept, away from China and through Mongolia. I looked out at the Gobi Desert, which was sliding by the windows, pressing my fingertips to the glass, trying to grasp at the disappearing threads of the dream: the girl, the track, her grief, my overwhelming compulsion to help her. The sky outside the window was vast, prickling with starlight, the vista so enormous I fancied it was almost possible to see the curvature of the earth.

I remember thinking, as I stood there, alone in the desert night, that the child must have been me: she looked, from the back, just as I had done, with her slight frame, her pale hair, her outpourings of emotion. I must, I reasoned, have been trying to catch up with a younger version of myself, to comfort her, to tell her that everything was going to be all right. But was it? I asked myself, as I gazed out at the desert. Was it going to be all right? I had no idea.

I believed this interpretation for years: that these nightly visions were a subconscious meeting between my adult and child self. Now, though, I wonder if it wasn't my daughter ahead of me there on the path.

She and I share certain physical characteristics; our likeness is often commented upon, by friends and strangers alike. Photographs of us at the same age could be interchangeable, if you ignore the 1970s nylon outfits I've been zipped into. A shaky, discoloured film of me, age five, at a street party, made her once exclaim, with absolute conviction, "There's me."

I've never had those dreams since. They vanished, evaporated, along with the other ephemera of my twenties:

the dreary rental flats, the uncertain and mind-shrivelling jobs, the late-night urban wanderings, the last buses, the monthly travel passes, the skipped meals, the ill-judged boyfriends, the pressing calls made from phone-boxes, the clothes (the insubstantial dresses, the T-shirts so short as to display the whole midriff, the trousers that rode low on the hipbones), the sincere and strenuous efforts to persuade adults older than you that you indeed could do what they needed, you definitely could, you were sure you could, all you needed was the chance.

Did my daughter appear to me a decade and a half before she was born? I like to think so. There she was, looping back through time to brush past a person not yet ready to be her mother—nowhere near ready, if I'm honest—tipping me the wink that she would one day arrive in my life. Readying me, perhaps, for the road ahead, sowing the seeds for all the strength, compassion and resilience required for her existence.

It's hard to articulate the level of care and patience required to look after a child with chronic eczema. These are children who are distressed and uncomfortable every minute of every day. They don't sleep, they can't eat, they can't play. They find clothing unbearable. Everything makes them itch—heat, cold, wool, sofas, animals, wind, grass, leaves, food, toys, perfume, soap, smoke, sand, concrete, mud, water, juice, ropes, elastic, clothes, dust, mould. They cannot concentrate on anything for longer than a second or two because the pain of their skin is so extreme, so distracting.

I have never known anything like it. I had not thought such suffering, such torture, was possible. Walking around the rooms of my house, holding this miserable, wailing baby, I had no idea what to do. I put on the ointments given to me by the doctor but they didn't work—they didn't even come close. I couldn't believe such a condition was allowed, that such a thing could happen. What, I wanted to howl to the walls, to the carpets, to the chairs, the hell do I do? I wanted to lodge a complaint, raise an objection, with somebody somewhere. I was frequently seized with an urge to run with her into the streets, to stop passers-by, to offer up my daughter to their gaze and say, look, do you see that? Have you ever known anything like it? Do you know what to do? Can you help her? Can you help me?

I had no idea how to live, how to be, how to bear witness to this level of agony in a child so young, how best to alleviate her pain.

I would put her down in her cot for a moment, so I could make a drink or a snack or even go to the toilet.

Halfway through this task, I would be summoned back by screams, to find that, in my brief absence, the bedding, the cot, the walls, the baby were now covered with blood because she had been driven to scratch herself, to tear off her clothes, to flay her own skin. I would lift her out, soothe her, cover her in emollient, put her into a clean outfit, change the sheets, load the soiled clothes and sheets into the washing-machine. I would try to stay calm, to remain positive. Look, I would say to her, laying her down on her play mat, a ball! A rattle! A lovely book, a squeaky duck! And then I would watch as she turned away, letting them fall from her fingers, curled into herself, started to rub her arms on the surface of the mat, seeking relief, seeking release, seeking any sensation other than the misery of her condition.

The day after the awful appointment with the consultant dermatologist, I am, for the twentieth or thirtieth time that morning, trying to smear my daughter with cream so that she can manage a feed, when Constance phones.

"I've found out who you need to see," she says. "He's called Dr. Fox and you'll have to pay, but he's the best. Everyone says so."

"I don't know," I mumble, tossing bottles and pots of lotion back into the basket under the sofa. "Private health-care, I'm just not sure if—"

Constance interrupts: "You can't go on like this. And neither can she."

I look down into my daughter's face, at her sentient blue gaze, at her broken and inflamed cheeks and forehead, at the infected and weeping skin of her neck, at the blood-stained sleepsuit.

I take down the number. I make the appointment. I pay the two hundred pounds. Within days, we are sitting in front of Dr. Fox (no waiting list, no unexplained delays). He asks about my daughter's birth, her diet, my medical history, my husband's. He smiles at my son, who is sitting in the room with us, and says, "No eczema there, I see." He asks me to undress my daughter and when I do his face turns carefully expressionless, professionally contemplative. He lifts her arms, he examines her wrists, her legs, her torso, handling her with the gentlest of touches.

He writes a list of what we should use: bath oils, soap substitutes, steroids, moisturisers, anti-bacterial ointments, detergent-free shampoo. He refers us to his NHS clinic so that we won't have to pay next time. He gives me a sheaf of leaflets about sensitive skins, sun-creams, laundry, specialist eczema clothing, silk gloves, closed-end pyjamas.

I am thanking him, getting up to leave, when he says, "I'd like to run some allergy tests. Just in case."

I'm taken aback. I almost say, let's not bother. Allergies

haven't been mentioned before now, by any of the other NHS medics she has seen. She has, so far, consumed only milk and a bit of puréed vegetable. Allergies are not on my radar. I don't have any and neither does my husband or my son. But because this doctor has been so good, so attentive, so careful with my daughter, I say yes. Of course I do. What other choice do I have?

I don't need to say, do I, that the tests came up positive, instantly and unequivocally? That she was allergic to a long list of things, several of which could tip her into dangerous, lethal anaphylaxis. That in the graphs, her Immunoglobulin E levels were registering up in the grey areas, the off-the-scale areas, the worse-than-severe. That in that moment our lives tilted to a new angle. That, looking at the results, I couldn't believe I'd been walking around the world with her in a state of horrible ignorance. (But I took her to Africa, to a remote Swedish island, I wanted to shriek, as if volume alone could retrospectively undo these acts.) That, within minutes, we were in a room with a training nurse who was showing my husband and me how to inject adrenalin into the thigh of a rubber doll.

The effects of living with a child who has a life-threatening condition, of loving someone who could, at any moment, be snatched from you? I think about this a lot.

Your lives are conducted with a constant background hum of potential peril. You begin to experience the world differently. You may no longer go for a walk and see a garden, a playground, a farm full of goat kids. You must always be tabulating and assessing risk: that pollinating silver birch, those food wrappers in the rubbish bin, those flowering nut trees, those gambolling dogs, shedding their dander and fur into the air. You school yourself, quickly, to keep your anxiety, your levels of vigilance tamped down, concealed, to maintain calm, to speak in a modulated voice, even when you are so gripped with panic that you can't hear anything other than your pounding heart. On seeing the approach of someone holding a chocolate hazelnut dip, you say—lightly, evenly—let's go over here, when part of you really wants to scream, run, run for your life.

You become ferociously, uncharacteristically organised: there are prescription lists to update, expiry dates to note down, letters to write, governmental departments to phone, internet searches to conduct, medication to be filed and bagged, symptoms and triggers to be recorded, forms to fill, receptionists to call, medical papers, reports and trials to keep abreast with, appointments to make, medical kits to be taken out of one handbag and stashed in another because what you must never, ever do is leave the house without it.

You perfect an excellent poker face for when doctors are delivering dreadful news in the presence of your child. You learn, quickly, to bring headphones and audiobooks to all hospital appointments so that you can clamp them over your child's ears and tune her into *The BFG* instead of whatever it is the doctor is about to say. You learn to say thank you, over and over again: to receptionists, to nurses, to doctors, to orderlies, to the people who bring the tea trolley, to the people who empty the sharps bins.

You make sure you say goodbye, properly and with eye contact, every time your child leaves the house. You will have trouble letting go of her hand sometimes, at the school gate, but you tell yourself to woman up, to hide this at all costs. You will find it hard to throw out anything your child has drawn or made or loved; you will spend time hesitating over rubbish bins or charity-shop piles before deciding, no, you cannot part with that unevenly glued owl, that much-worn fox, no matter how overstuffed your cupboards are.

You worry—a lot—about what effect all this has on her, on her psyche, on her stress levels. You yourself know that a near-death experience changes you forever: you come back from the brink altered, wiser, sadder. You wonder what she is thinking, where she goes, when she feels her airways closing in, when she hears the distant wail of the ambulance, when she sees her mother bearing down on her with a syringe, when she registers the jolt of the adrenalin reaching her bloodstream. You know that any journey like this to the edge of the abyss marks a child out, makes her different. There is nothing you can do about it, of course, but still you worry. You worry what effect it will have on sibling dynamics. You don't ever want her brother and sister to feel overlooked, overshadowed or—Heaven forbid—resentful towards her. You worry.

You are desperate for people to see the person beyond the condition, for her to be viewed as more than just a collection of symptoms. Too often her eczema, her allergies, her sudden spikes of illness are seen as a synecdoche for her, for the child she is. You hear someone at the school gates refer to her as "the girl with the gloves" and you want to go to them and say, tell me what else about her you can see.

You want her to be recognised as a person, not just a medical phenomenon. You begin to hate the word "problem": what she has aren't "problems"; she herself isn't a "problem" and neither is her presence in a room. You spend a long time compiling lists of acceptable words before settling on "challenge." You try it out: my child has immunology challenges; she has dermatological challenges.

You pretend not to notice, not to care, when the height and weight charts tell you she hasn't grown at all in the past year. You reel off positive synonyms for the word "small," when she wonders why everyone in her class is taller than her: petite, you tell her, neat, compact, dainty, diminutive, perfect.

You will, for a while, expend some time and energy into finding out why this has happened. Why her? Some theories put to you by various practitioners include: the amalgam fillings in your molars, her conception via IVF, the loss of the other embryo and how this must have felt like losing a skin, a previous life trauma (for her or for you was never clear), a tetanus jab you had while unknowingly pregnant with her, an unnaturally clean house (this one makes you laugh), the confluence of your mild asthma and your husband's occasional eczema, and so on. You decide to give up on the why and instead concentrate on the how.

There are times when everything takes on shades of mythology: you hold up her adrenalin injectors to the light, pondering that clearish yellow liquid, and realise that you have been given an elixir to bring your child back from death. You must stab her to save her. You can haul her back from the dark, but only if you have the right collection of items, only if you make an appeal to the right person. There are times when you chide yourself for being too fanciful. And then, when you are reading the story of Persephone to your daughter, you can't quite believe how pertinent it is, and you wonder what people knew of this then. You and your daughter turn to face each other wordlessly, absorbing the tale of the girl who ate six fateful seeds, condemning herself to the underworld, and the mother who fought to bring her back.

You will take your children to a museum of anthropology, and you will gaze down at eighteenth-century amulets from Papua New Guinea, worn to ward off evil spirits, death, disease. Several are the circumference of a child's wrist. A familiar commingling of hope, desperation and an urge to protect rises from beads, twine and feathers. You think: you too? You think: did it work? You are seized with the desire to slip your hand under the glass, take one, attach it to your child, to all your children, and walk quickly away.

You will become a person who can say to a beloved child, everything is okay, when you know that, just behind that curtain, someone is preparing a scalpel, which will shortly be used to drain an abscess on her leg. You will be the one who holds her down. It will be your hands on her knees, on her arms; it will be your torso pinning down hers. It will be your voice speaking over her screams, trying to reassure, trying to tell her it will soon be over.

You learn to smile distantly when people say, ooh, I don't know how you cope. You learn that there will be days when the responsibility, the limitations, the threat feel overwhelming, devastating. At these times, you must take yourself off somewhere, far away from anyone else, somewhere you can cry and mutter to yourself. You will go on a course to learn how to do CPR, and as you pound the mechanical heart of the faceless dummy, counting down from fifteen, you think, one day this could be my child.

You will find reservoirs of strength you didn't know you had. You will find friends who say, of course she can come over, I'll vacuum and clean and wipe the house in preparation, I'll scrub the tables, I'll make eggless cookies, I'll do anything at all, tell me what to do. You will be bowled over by kindness more times than you will be felled by callousness. You will think at times that you can't bear it, but you do.

You grow a thick skin for the mothers at playgrounds who look at your child's chronic eczema and say loudly, in her full hearing, "What's wrong with her? Is it catching?" You will turn your face away when someone tells you they're not inviting her to a birthday party because "it's too much hassle."

You will become so grateful towards people who show kindness and compassion to her that it will be hard for you to hold yourself in check. You have to tell yourself to be sensible, unemotional, when you encounter these terrestrial angels, not to embrace them with alarming intensity, not to thank them repeatedly. Keep it light, you warn yourself, when you see the teacher who insisted that your child be accepted for a place, despite the extra work this entails; the pharmacist who took one look at her and authorised an order for protective dermatological bodysuits, even though the GP deemed them too expensive. A woman in a department-store changing room who said nothing when blood soaked through your child's clothes to leave stains on the seat. An allergy nurse who is willing to write letters for you, to lobby schools and education authorities for you, to come with open arms to the door of the ambulance when your child arrives in the throes of anaphylaxis.

You will want nothing more for your child, for all your children, than for them to live their lives unencumbered by worry, by discomfort, by the judgement of others. You will go to bed at night and breathe into the dark and think, one more day. I kept her alive for one more day.

You will not be fazed by tonsillitis, by appendicitis, by a child soaked to the skin at the beginning of a long walk, by vomit, by grazed knees, by splinters, by dungarees encrusted with dog shit, by hair stealthily slicked back with yoghurt just as you are about to board an international flight, by a lake of shampoo squeezed out onto the bathroom floor, by A and E visits for stitches and sprains and concussion, by crayon on newly painted walls, by rain coming through the roof of your house, by a learner driver wrecking the car. This stuff is small; life is large.

In Italy, we have driven down a road that has petered out into a rough, pebbled track. Will has reversed the car, silently, grimly, and sped back the other way. This second route seems to be narrowing down as well, the road surface becoming bumpier, the trees leaning closer. I am no longer meeting Will's eyes in the rear-view mirror. I am looking only at my daughter, holding her close to me, as if this could make any difference. She is noticeably weaker, paler, still wheezing and clawing at her throat; my other children are subdued, silent.

Suddenly, from the dashboard, the satnav gives a loud beep. The screen flashes on, then off, and a map appears, the roads in white, the fields in green. We have contact. There is, it's showing us, a junction up ahead and, several turnings away, a main road: beautifully straight, mercifully wide.

We are, the satnav informs us, with its inimitable, electronic calm, two minutes from the *autostrada* and eight minutes from a hospital. A red "H" is surging on and off in the corner of a screen as we drive, beaming us in, guiding us down: eight minutes away, seven, six. Will accelerates down the *autostrada*, speed limits be damned, and when we get to Orvieto Hospital, we will screech in at the ambulance-only entrance and I will leap out, already sprinting, my daughter held before me, like an offering. I will be thinking, oh no you don't. Not now, not here. You're not getting her, not today, not any time soon.

She is, she is, she is.

Acknowledgements

Thank you, Will Sutcliffe.

Thank you Mary-Anne Harrington and Victoria Hobbs.

Thank you Cathie Arrington, Sarah Badhan, Yeti Lambregts, Georgina Moore, Hazel Orme, Vicky Palmer, Amy Perkins, Barbara Ronan and all at Tinder Press. Thank you Jennifer Custer, Vickie Dillon, Hélène Ferey and all at A.M. Heath.

Thank you to my parents, for answering questions and providing documents; to my sister, for sharing her recollections of our childhood; to Sarah Urwin Jones, for reassuring conversations about the nature of memoir; to Ruth Metzstein, for yet another inimitable last-draft steer; to Professor Rustam Al-Shahi Salman, for neurological editing and advice.

I am forever grateful to the following people for their expertise, compassion and support for my daughter:

Dr. Adam Fox (who will always be known in our house as Fantastic Dr. Fox), Professor Jürgen Schwarze, Susan Brown, Sister Lowe and the team at Lauriston Place Dermatology Department, Daisy Donovan, Francisca Morton, Susana Montoya-Peláez, Charlotte Willson, Lorna Wills, Vivienne Mackay and Karen Ford. You have, each and every one of you, made an enormous difference to her life.

From the proceeds of this book, a donation will be made to the following charities: the Anaphylaxis Campaign, who support and lobby for those with severe allergies; Medical Alert Dogs, who train dogs to assist and protect people living with life-threatening medical conditions.

Illustration Credits

A NOTE ABOUT THE AUTHOR

Born in Northern Ireland in 1972, Maggie O'Farrell grew up in Wales and Scotland. She is the author of seven novels, *After You'd Gone* (2000), *My Lover's Lover* (2002), *The Distance Between Us* (2004), *The Vanishing Act of Esme Lennox* (2006), *The Hand That First Held Mine* (2010), which won the Costa Novel Award, *Instructions for a Heatwave* (2013) and, most recently, *This Must Be the Place* (2016). She lives in Edinburgh.